OPEN
WITH A
CLOSE

THE TWELVE-POINT GUIDE TO
CLOSING MORE SALES

MATTHEW ELWELL

R3THINK PRESS

First published in Great Britain in 2020
by Rethink Press (www.rethinkpress.com)

Praise

'I love the way Matt teaches sales. He brings a vast depth of knowledge and experience to the table but, more then that, his OWAC method has heart. He cares.'
   —**Veronica Pullen,** CEO of Mile Deep Marketing

'Having spent most my working life in a corporate role – albeit many of those years in the motor trade – I'd never had to sell. So when I started my own business, I not only didn't know how to sell, but I realised my mindset around sales was unhelpful. Matt and Open With A Close have changed all that, helping me see that selling is serving and giving me the tools to do this at the very highest level. He really is the master and I'd highly recommend anyone who hates selling to go see Matt – I can guarantee he'll change your mind.'
   —**Sally Wright,** Sally Dreams Photography

'Since discovering Matt and his OWAC method, not only have I become a much more shrewd negotiator (on all things in life, not just in work scenarios) but the impact of the new language I've learned continues to benefit me and my family on a daily basis.'
   —**Adam Ashburn,** Operations Director at Expert Empires

Contents

*I would like to dedicate this book to my family:
my mom and dad, Sandra and Phil; my sister, Tamar;
my brother, Marcus.*

*And in particular to my wonderful wife, Kerry, who is
my most loyal partner, friend and mother and has
such a beautiful soul; and to my amazing
daughters, Olivia Rose and Eva Lily.*

Finally, to my amazing business partner, Nick James.

What a phenomenal time to be alive!

Foreword

I count myself fortunate to have been trained and mentored by some truly amazing people. At just twelve years of age I attended my first seminar with the legendary Tony Robbins, in Hawaii. Thanks to my mum's obsession with personal development, I was raised in an environment of world-class coaches and speakers.

In my early twenties I worked closely with Andy Harrington as he built his first neurolinguistic programming (NLP) training company. More recently, as I have developed my own events company, I have partnered with some of the world's best-known influencers and celebrity entrepreneurs: people such as Grant Cardone, Lord Alan Sugar, Gary Vaynerchuk, David Goggins and Lewis Howes.

Despite the vast amount of knowledge I have accumulated over the last twenty-four years, I can honestly say that Matthew Elwell's training has been as impactful as anything I have ever experienced.

Matthew and I have known each other since we were kids, but it was only in October 2017 that we started working together in a professional capacity. He had recently sold his stake in the family business, and felt compelled to explore the world of coaching and training.

Knowing of my industry experience, Matthew connected with me on Facebook, and one night we met up for a beer. After the usual chit-chat, we began to discuss possible ways for us to work together and collaborate. Within minutes I could sense that Matthew had a rare talent – one that my business could benefit from massively – and so I quickly contracted him to consult for my company.

In no time at all, Matthew's teachings and philosophies made a significant impact on me and my sales team. We literally doubled our sales conversions in less than a week. As months passed, that impact continued to spread through my entire company like wildfire. My staff, clients, event delegates, partners and stakeholders all began to benefit from Matthew's teachings.

Fast-forward eighteen months, and my company has seen an additional £1.2 million in sales revenue as a direct result of the work that Matthew has done within my business. The increase in sales for my clients is quite frankly impossible for me to measure, but I would conservatively estimate a minimum of £10 million, probably more.

In August 2018 Matthew and I co-founded the Elite Closing Academy – a company which now delivers what I consider to be *the best* training on the planet when it comes to selling and closing. The core philosophies that our clients spend thousands of pounds to learn have been documented for you here in this book.

Make no mistake about it. The body of work you are holding in your hands right now is powerful beyond measure. The lessons you are about to learn have the potential to change your business, your income and your life, forever.

All you need to do now is read, absorb and implement – and wait for the magic to happen!

To your success,

Nick James
Creator of Expert Empires, CEO of Seriously Fun Business Ltd, and Co-founder of the Elite Closing Academy

Introduction

Just about everywhere I go in business and in life, and whenever I get talking to business owners of all sizes – entrepreneurs, consultants, experts, shop owners, retail businesses, martial arts centre owners, gyms, coaches, car salespeople, bar managers, wait staff, friends, family, tour operators, committee members of clubs that I'm in, to name just a few – a few common themes about 'selling' exist.

First, that virtually no one is terribly good at it. Second, that no one seems to be able to differentiate between selling and closing: they are two totally different things. Third, that no one seems to understand how to prospect properly. By this I mean asking, serving and nurturing to ensure that there is a potential future, even if there is no current apparent need. Finally, that the fear of selling, or being sold to, is so raw that you can almost touch it.

We have a universal fear of being sold to and selling.

This book sets out my unique, twelve-step process to close more business in a way that is congruent with you, your personal values and business's purpose, with a human-to-human approach.

Mastering the techniques in this book involves you and your team being able to prospect and qualify potential clients (prospects) by moving them along your pipeline, so that eventually, on receipt of all the data and with an emotional attachment to your products or services, they pop out of the sales cycle as a hot qualified lead ready to be closed, using my Open With A Close (OWAC) method.

Once mastered, my everyday saying – 'What a phenomenal time to be alive!' – will strike a chord within you, as you watch your business grow both online and offline, and see your business relationships improve, bringing a crucial cycle – the Close Yourself Cycle – to life. Certainty is the thing that will make the difference, and that comes from within. This is my most advanced sales technique, which involves prospects coming *towards* you, your products and services, because they have decided that you are the solution to their problems, pain or needs. They believe that you will get them a result.

I believe that I was born to teach my sales and closing philosophy. The first thirty-nine years of my life were the breeding ground of my teachings now, which are based on experiences in business, sport, teamwork, human interaction, long-standing relationships, influencing and working towards the logical next step with every situation.

When I first started sales consulting for my business partner and great friend Nick James, co-founder of the Elite Closing Academy and creator of Expert Empires, I was humbled that my training was impacting deeply on business results and patterns of language and behaviour within people and, ultimately, teams. I found understanding the impact terribly difficult at first, and harder to take credit for even better results. I now understand how important it is to celebrate the success that we achieve with our clients, and to put it on the record to assist others when making informed decisions.

I also take extremely seriously the power of impact and change that my training has on humans. It's my duty. It's my responsibility. It's the reason why I created the Elite Closing Academy as a learning tool, via world-class training and coaching to salespeople and teams all over the globe, to assist them on the journey to becoming 'Elite Closers'.

This book is not for when you are in the prospecting cycle. This book is not for cold traffic. *Open With A Close* is specifically designed for closing hot, qualified leads.

Before We Start...

Before we can delve into closing hot, qualified leads, there are two important principles to understand:

1. Serve, Sell, Close: the Serve Circle

2. The Prospecting Journey: from caterpillar egg to beautiful butterfly (CEBB)

Serve, Sell, Close: the Serve Circle

A common problem I find in salespeople, investors and entrepreneurs is an inability to grasp the difference between serving, selling and closing and, more often, forgetting one of them altogether during the sales process.

Each of the elements in the Serve Circle are important: you can't bypass any of them, or only be good at one of them. You have to understand and use each element during the process.

The Serve Circle

When salespeople don't understand this circle, they make one of three major mistakes.

1. Serving without selling or closing

Serving prospects by giving them lots of your time, ample information and often minute details is definitely important, but it requires discipline. If you overserve, forget to sell and try to close, it feels uncomfortable. You leave people wondering what they should do next, and what the point of all that information was.

2. Sell, sell, sell

Some salespeople sell, sell, sell – they bombard the prospect with lots of features and benefits, never letting them speak or ask any questions. They then try to close without ever serving. These guys also use presumption and assumption a lot, blasting out phrases such as: 'people like you'. Not good.

3. Closing without selling or serving

Plenty of salespeople try to close without selling, and with little serving.

Worst of all, many salespeople try to serve, sell and close at the same time. You know the ones: 'Let's meet for coffee, I won't try to sell you anything,' or, 'It's just a quick call, I'm not trying to sell anything.' These salespeople get disheartened when, at the slightest glimmer of interest from the prospect, they rush into a big, hyped-up pitch, loaded with features and benefits, and try to collude, persuade or even push the prospect into making a decision that just doesn't feel right there and then.

The prospect's only way out, maintaining politeness, is to say:

It's interesting, I just need to think about it.

Or:

*It's really interesting, I just need you to pop it on
an email.*

Or:

*I would love to, but I need to check with the board
[or my business partner].*

These are all code for:

*Back off! You have not earned the right to ask me a
closing question.*

The Serve Circle is about balance, the perfect blend of:

- High-calibre service

- Selling by asking world-class, powerful questions

- Understanding by following my PUNT with a Q
  system: Pain–Urgency–Need–Trust Quantitative
  (see Chapter 1)

- Making a meaningful written proposal

- Knowing the exact moment to stop selling and
  start closing

– all of which make for the highest level of service you
can give another business or person.

**Serve unconditionally. Selling is serving. Closing is
serving.**

A question you might have right now is: 'How do I know when to transition from serving to selling to closing?'

A rule I teach in the Serve Circle is when prospects ask 'How does it work?', that is the time to begin the transition from serving to selling. Then – only after you have made a written proposal that takes into account their pain, challenges, urgency, needs, understanding, quantitative data and trust – can you begin the closing phase. (If you don't have the opportunity to make a written proposal, at least make a verbal offer.)

Now, you can get into the Serve, Sell, Close cycle only if you have a prospect. Let's look at the Prospecting Journey.

The Prospecting Journey: from caterpillar egg to beautiful butterfly (CEBB)

Do you know how much contact you need to have with someone before they are ready to buy from you? Internationally, the sweet spot is between five and twelve times. It is critical to have data relating to the average amount of contact you have with your prospects before they actually buy from you.

Go and work it out now, and note this figure for the future.

What is a contact?

A contact can be, to name just a few:

- A click on an advert
- Website visit (as long as you have collected the visitor's details)
- Phone call
- Meeting
- Email response
- Text
- Facebook message
- Written proposal

A caterpillar takes time to transition into a beautiful butterfly. A prospect, just like a little caterpillar egg, needs time to be at a point in the sales cycle to transition into a paying customer: closed. This principle is important, so that you and your team prepare quality contact on the customer's journey within your community.

It also alters the sales mindset. The chrysalis cannot be forced to break and the insect to start flapping its wings, in much the same way that a prospect who has only just found out about your products or services cannot make an informed buying decision on the spot, just because you have given them all the features and benefits of what it is you would do for them!

The key principle here is: **nurture your prospects** from the front end of your pipeline, and always look to provide enough information and gain enough understanding to move them along it. That is the logical next step.

It also means that when you first meet or talk to someone, please do not expect to close them there and then. Instead, be obsessed with what information they might need about how your service could possibly overcome the problems or challenges they face in business, linked to what you do. Serve unconditionally and obsessively!

- Find out what they have seen or heard about your products or services that, when implemented in their business, would get them even better results or solve their problems.

- Ask them about their challenges, pain and problems. Quantify and measure as much as possible.

- Find out how critical their challenges are to resolve right now.

- What will happen if they don't solve them?

- Find out what they need to solve those challenges and problems.

- Gain huge trust along the journey.

Once armed with all the data – the truth – you can make your decision as a salesperson. Do we have a genuine solution to this business or person's problems? Yes or no? If 'Yes', find out:

1. What the decision-making process is

2. Who is involved in the process

3. What the key buying criteria are

4. Who makes the ultimate decision

5. How long they would need to decide

6. The deciding process and key factors

7. The possible risks, implications, pitfalls or obstacles

8. The key results they would need for this to be the greatest investment they have ever made in the business

9. A locked-down time to speak via Zoom, Skype, face to face or over the phone

Once you have all of this data – and only at this point – should you **make a written proposal.** Lock down the next logical step, and you're in business to close the next time you speak.

If it's a 'No' for now, here are some useful steps to follow. You can say:

> *I understand it's not right for you now. When would be the right time?*

How would you prefer for us to stay in touch in the future, or not at all? (Clean up your pipeline.)

With which medium would you prefer for us to communicate: free information, or not at all?

And refer them to someone you know who could help them. Then you can ask them for a referral for you:

Who else do you know who might possibly need what we do now?

Simple!

Key note

Every one of the outcomes below is a good result when prospecting. *You cannot fail when following this process.*

Four outcomes from prospecting:

1. Yes, we definitely need this *now*.

2. Yes, very interesting. We need more information and a written proposal, to possibly involve other decision-makers, and then lock another time down to close the deal.

3. Great making contact, we have no immediate need but would like to stay in your community for another time. (Get a referral and grow your community.)

4. 'F**k Off and Die' (FOAD) – unsubscribe me.
   (This is a good result, because it keeps your
   pipeline clean. Oh, and ask for a cheeky referral.)

Three-phase process for all sales conversations

Every time I enter into a sales conversation, I follow this simple, three-phase process. I follow and trust it unequivocally.

QUALIFY – Phase 1

Confirm that you have the correct person.

Qualify them by asking the Problem question (Prospecting Pain Question – P.P.Q.).

Transition into Phase 2 – the link is: 'First, thank you...'

THEM – Phase 2

Ask Brain 2 and 3 questions where required and depending on where you are on the Prospecting Journey (Serve, Sell, Close – the Serve Circle).

Transition into Phase 3 – the link is: 'Here's what I suggest happens next...'

US – Phase 3

Closing questions only (Close cycle).

Lock down the logical next step, to move the situation along your pipeline.

In this book we're focusing on Us – Phase 3. I'm going to show you how to use the twelve-step OWAC method.

Part One will cover some really useful foundations to get your thinking right. Your mindset is your greatest tool, so we'll get you into a great frame of mind to close more deals. In Part Two we'll delve into the twelve-step OWAC methodology that I have created and used successfully for more than twenty years. We'll look at:

- Handling objections

- Red and green words

- The 3As (Agree, Appease, Accelerate) when closing

- The Bullseye technique

– and loads more.

By the end of this book you will have your own bespoke script for closing more deals.

PART ONE
THE FOUNDATIONS

1
Thoughts

Everyone has a marketing strategy, with a system that creates loads of leads. Everyone has a website, social media, funnels, LinkedIn profile, Facebook account and networking meetings to attend. Everyone has a recruitment strategy, with a system in place to employ people. Everyone has a financial director or 'money person' who has a strategy for saving, investing and spending. Everyone has a serve strategy for existing customers.

The same cannot be said for a sales strategy. Yes, most businesses have a 'strategy', but:

- How often is it reviewed?

- What are the actual numbers?

- What results are you achieving?

- Where could you possibly improve?

- How often do you invest time and money in training both yourself and your staff to be world-class at selling?

- Who in your organisation closes the business created by salespeople?

- How many of your other staff have 'sales' training?

Our attitudes towards sales and money are formed from our youth and our parents' attitude towards money. Think about some of the money lessons you learned from your parents or carers, grandparents or schoolteachers. It was probably about saving money, not talking about how much you had, pretending you didn't have much. These attitudes all have negative connotations.

When you were young, who said to you how great it was to have lots of spare cash to invest in yourself, your family, business, community or future? Was there anyone in your environment who had great thoughts about money and sales? These ingrained little money and sales patterns may explain the reason why businesses never seem to put the same amount of time and effort into a sales strategy, and why so many people move away from the sales process.

Some businesses have been ordinary at selling for years. They constantly invest in internet marketing, Facebook ads, etc, but this doesn't solve the problem because at some point, if a prospect that is created online doesn't convert online ('abandoned cart'), they still need to be closed by a human being. They still have the problem that attracted them to your products or services in the first place, but they haven't been closed, therefore we have not 'served' them properly.

The opposite of 'close' is 'open'.

By not having the skills to close professionally, you leave your prospect in need and open-ended. How much time, effort and money have been wasted creating an attraction via social media or online to your business, then the prospect never buys from you due to a lack of skill in closing the sale? In fact, **people actively avoid the sales process** at times. Even experienced salespeople seem to spend more time checking notes, emailing, writing proposals, using social media, making excuses and generally busying themselves with everything except getting on the phone, making face-to-face appointments to present proposals, finding new business contacts and closing deals.

What about a fresh leads strategy? How much actual training does the sales team get, how much energy goes into new business, how many cold calls do they make? How many follow-ups are they making to clients that used you recently or in the past, purchased a low-priced product, went to a seminar, read a book, watched a webinar, visited your website, left a message on your Facebook page, or that you have quoted in the past but lost out?

How much energy is going into sales that are not 'low-hanging fruit'? The hard 'yakka'. The 50/50s that need nurturing, hard high-quality questions and a deeper understanding of the clients' needs. The bottom line is that so many people in business and life avoid salespeople, sales conversations and the hard work required to create new sales leads. For many people, a perception of confrontation, fear and rejection exists.

Recall a bad sales experience you've had. Perhaps it was a car salesperson, window salesperson, door knocker, phone call about insurance at 8pm, a retail shop, a restaurant whose staff were rigid with no flexibility for your requests – these experiences shape your view and thinking of any sales experience you're going to have. Recall how uncomfortable the hard sell felt. When they were talking over you, talking far too much, trying to persuade you of all the features and benefits, the sales pitch, the presumption of your needs without asking, the total lack of understanding of what you or your business actually needs right now to grow, not listening to what you say and, most annoyingly, saying 'No' to you.

Most business people that I meet have a great product – often, a phenomenal business – but all share a deep-rooted fear of rejection. They struggle to keep turning new business leads into paying customers.

The great news is that I know what this feels like, and have created a simple, easy-to-follow solution which, when mastered and repeated, produces consistent results. This system is proven to work in many different industries, including:

- Sales

- Property negotiation

- Retail sales

- Commercial sales

- The car industry

- Corporate sales

- Health and well-being

- Service industry

- Call centres

- Martial arts

- Dentists

- Gyms

- Live events on stage and at the back of the room

- Showrooms

- PowerPoint presentations

- One-to-one consultations

- Facebook lives

- Webinars

- Follow-ups over the phone

- Group meetings

– and many more.

It has also proven to work in Germany, Ireland, the Netherlands, Scotland, Switzerland, the USA, Wales and many other countries.

I have experience in the photocopying industry, cold calling, door knocking and sales training, and ran my own retail business dealing with the general public, selling face to face. I currently teach my techniques to live audiences, large and small groups and to a few hand-selected private clients at our amazing training centre in Solihull and online. I know what it's like to sell products starting from £5 up to millions. I have negotiated and closed everything from £2.99 for a bag of tile spacers, all the way up to a multi-seven-figure property deal.

I also navigated the great crash in 2008–10, so I understand what it feels like to have made a huge investment in a business, only to be faced with crippling overheads, unmotivated and stressed staff, lack of sales, appalling cash flow and the real possibility of losing everything that my family and I had created. I know what it takes to trade and break out the other end through really difficult times. I understand business, entrepreneurial human beings and individuals who want to sell for themselves or within organisations, and I understand teams of salespeople because I have experienced it for myself with my own and other people's staff.

All strategies are not the same

People often ask me what is different about my strategy and techniques. Well, I advocate two extremely powerful processes around sales:

1. We should use our hearts, and our heads, when selling

2. Serve, Sell, Close – **the Serve Circle**

Understanding the nuances required is critical to a perfect sales process. The skill is twofold:

1. Mastering the idea that quality selling is *asking*, as opposed to *telling*

2. Knowing when to transition from serving to selling, and selling to closing

This is one of the first trainings I do as a foundation in my live training, because once you grasp this everything you do in the sales process changes:

THE ELITE CLOSING ACADEMY CORE MINDSET

Selling is serving. Closing is serving. Serving is serving (unconditional).

To really understand this powerful cycle, it is worth considering the opposites of the words above:

- The opposite of serve is to *hold back*

- The opposite of sell is to *get*

- The opposite of close is *open*

Many salespeople are focused on *get*. They want to get a sale, get a commission, get the answer that their rhetorical question obviously gives, get a holiday, get a new car. All this 'get' energy is about themselves and what they want, not about the prospect and how they can serve them.

My concern for many of the sales teams I encounter is that often a deal that should have been closed, or a prospect that falls into the category of your perfect customer, ends up not doing the deal or buying your product or service because a member of the sales team was in *get* energy. They are more focused on their own outcome, as opposed to really understanding what the prospect needs and then following the tried-and-tested process to the close.

The consequences of this typical sales mindset are that the prospect feels hard sold to – and this is the moment when a salesperson starts telling the prospect what they think they should do, and all the reasons why the prospect would be stupid not to do it.

Features and benefit-selling lives here. Stop it!

This is where assumption and presumption dwell, and they are not helpful to a salesperson. To serve unconditionally, you need to get clear on the pain you are solving and become a master *pain* solver.

Red and green words

I recall on one of our core training events in Solihull, that Dee was working on her closing script. She was getting frustrated. I helped Dee understand the difference between red words and green words. Dee was only talking in green words (her promises), and was missing out completely on the red words – the pain that her prospect would be feeling. Dee was speaking to her prospects at a surface level. She was using her head, not her heart.

When I helped her find the red 'heart' words that would connect with the prospect's emotional, spiritual, mental and physical pain, as well as the financial effects, she was able to write a script that would close. Her script was powered up by red and green language.

This concept of red and green words comes from the 'Map of Consciousness' created and published by Dr David R. Hawkins.[1] He explains the classification and characteristics of energy fields that are around us in our daily life. His research found that roughly 85% of the world tunes in to the eight stress channels: the red language of shame, guilt, apathy, grief, fear, desire, anger, pride. When you connect with people in the red world, with their pain, you can close more sales.

Red and green words are an Elite Closing Academy core language technique. Here are examples of common green words/phrases.

Green

- *Our programme can get you more sales*

- *We can help improve your mindset*

- *We will make you more productive*

- *We can make you more cost-effective*

- *We teach better culture*

---

1   David R. Hawkins (1995) Power vs Force: The hidden determinants of human behaviour. London: Hay House.

– all surface words that the brain cannot quantify or gather context on.

Red

Often it's the opposite of the green word that is the problem – it's your job to ask questions and find out:

- *By not getting enough sales now, what impact is that having on your bottom line?*

- *What area of mindset can you improve on?*

- *Other than the bottom-line issues, what other impact does 'not enough sales' have on you personally? On the team's culture? Other than money, how else does a lack of sales impact the business overall?*

- *What are the impacts and ramifications for you as the owner, and for your employees? Not only financially, but emotionally, spiritually, physically and mentally?*

- *What will you do if your business folds?*

- *How do the results affect your ability to make decisions?*

Can you see how you keep going down the chain of red thoughts until you get to the truth? The red words focus in on the consequences: they are deeper, critical to a business and can be the first time the prospect has really, deeply considered the consequences about what you are asking (selling) them. Often, it can be a breakthrough moment when a leader, owner or decision-maker actually stops to consider what's going on in their business, and that it needs to be sorted fast.

Ultimately, the consequences of not having yourself or your team highly skilled in these easily learned principles result in fewer conversions of the often-expensive and time-consuming leads generated.

This mentality shift is a game changer.

Remember, world-class selling is asking world-class questions linked to what you sell (these are outcome questions). All my teaching foundations start with this attitude.

I use **serving questions** such as:

> *What information can I send you for free, right now?*
>
> *If there was one training I could give you that helps, what would it be?*

I use **selling questions** linked to my outcome, such as:

> *When it comes to your sales process and closing deals, what would you say is your biggest closing challenge right now?*

What is it about our products or services that, when implemented in your business, would get you an even better result – or maybe solve a problem?

I use **closing questions** such as:

Thank you, there are two dates to get started, [X] or [Y] – which one works for you?

What are the sixteen digits across your card, and I will lock the date down?

Where shall I send the invoice to be paid?

How quickly would you like to get this solved?

My teaching is based on an authentic, human approach from the heart, and the head. It does not involve hard, aggressive sales tactics – they're not required, and my technique avoids persuasion. My OWAC system enables people to see for themselves that your product or service is the right choice for them.

What's wrong with persuasion?

My golden rule has always been never to sell something to someone who doesn't want or need it. Get good at saying 'No' at the beginning if it is not a great match, and recommend a stakeholder of yours – and, of course, ask for a referral.

Knowing and understanding exactly what your potential customers want and need totally alters the sales process. It is so much easier to align a client with a product that they have identified as *needing*, than it is to try and sell them on the benefits that you think they need *without ever actually asking them*.

KEY POINT

Find out what your clients' needs are, before assuming or presuming that you know.

It's called Hard High-Quality Questioning and listening. How many of you reading this book are aware that you need to become a better listener, not just in business but also in life?

I have created several different strategies to do this, including Close Yourself, Hard High-Quality Questions, Denting and Elite Profiling to name just a few.

This book deals with the simplest way **to make more sales**, using:

- Helpful assumptions

- Knowledge of our brains

- An understanding of how human beings work when they are buying something

- Amazing rapport

- Simple but powerful language techniques

- Tonality

- A twelve-step closing system that can be used every time you are speaking to a prospect (either over the phone or face to face)

Take a PUNT With A Q

These Hard High-Quality Questions are used in my PUNT with a Q system:

Pain–Urgency–Need–Trust Quantitative

Great selling is all about asking great questions. You need to ask these to enable prospects to find the truth for themselves during the Prospecting Journey. Try asking five questions in each of these categories:

Pain

- *What results would you need to get in the first twelve weeks, for this to be the greatest investment you've ever made?*

- *What performance indicators would we need to put in place to ensure we are achieving improved results?*

- *How many more [XYZ] would you need to justify this investment?*

- *What financial implications are there now, as a result of not having [XYZ]?*

- *What have you seen or heard about us which, when executed in your business, would solve challenges or get even better results?*

Urgency

- *What is going to happen if you don't solve this?*

- *How critical is this to resolve right now?*

- *How many more [XYZ] would you need to get to solve this?*

- *How many months have you been experiencing this?*

- *How many more months can you afford to have this problem?*

Need

- *What do you think you need from us right now?*

- *If you could put your finger on the one thing you need to change, what would it be?*

- *What one thing must change in your view?*

- *If we could gift you a piece of information now that would help, what would it be?*

- *Other than money, what needs to change?*

Trust

- *Other than money, think of five other reasons why this would be a good deal.*

- *Who else would benefit?*

- *What do you know about our results with other people?*

- *Which one of our previous partners would you like me to put you in touch with, prior to us doing business together?*

- *Aside from money, what question can you ask about our company's values that is important for you to understand, before choosing us?*

Don't forget: whenever you ask powerful questions, it's important to find quantitative answers – things that you can measure. For example, if a prospect answers 'more leads' to a pain question about leads then ask: how many more, how many do you get now, what are they worth individually? Having exact data is always helpful during the prospecting cycle.

In short, OWAC comes from a position of **truth, not persuasion.** It gets to the point professionally, and qualifies your intentions right at the beginning of an interaction.

A reason for everything

I ask myself and those around me this question all the time: 'What's your strongest reason?'

- *What is your strongest reason for choosing this book?*

- *What is your strongest reason for starting this company?*

- *What is your strongest reason for wanting to change something?*

- *What is your strongest reason for wanting to be successful?*

- *What is your strongest reason for being a salesperson?*

- *If it was because you need more sales, ask yourself: what's my strongest reason for wanting more sales?*

Does this all sound a bit obvious? Knowing your strongest reason for anything is crucial, because you can gauge how much you are prepared to change, sacrifice or do differently to achieve your strongest reason goals.

KEY POINT

How much are you prepared to change, sacrifice or do differently to achieve your strongest reason goals?

Being successful and winning in sales is not easy. It requires you to make changes when they are needed, and to challenge your processes and procedures at all times. Standing still brings stagnation and, eventually, the end of your career in business. It's not an option. If you are one of the 'We've always done things this way' kind of people, then this book is not for you – or perhaps it will inspire you to think differently.

Understanding your purpose, your biggest why, *your strongest reason for doing what you do*, will help you stay on track when times are tough. Trust me: in sales, you will have good times and bad. It's how you deal with the bad, and how hard you focus when it's good, that separates the successful from the unsuccessful.

Finally, a powerful question to refocus your mind and remind you and your whole team of the company's purpose: the reason why you started up in the first place! If our business were not here today, who would be suffering right now? Who has the problem?

What's your strongest reason for starting your business?

The days of having a great concept, a fabulous business but not enough clients, or a sales team that is underperforming, are over for you – as long as you follow the advice in this book and challenge yourself to change your selling techniques, master the art of closing and overcome your fears.

Get out of your own way, rid yourself of ancient patterns that stop you, and step into certainty where all the money is. Stop being your own internal police force!

2

40,000 Brain Cells In Our Hearts?

Currently, everyone thinks that selling is all about social media – Facebook, Messenger, Twitter, web pages, Instagram, LinkedIn – but if you believe that, you are going to fail.

Of course, you need to use every platform there is to promote your business and sell yourself, your products and services, but the fact is that human beings are the most complex, amazing, intriguing and powerful beings on this planet. Humans purchase goods or services from other humans that they trust, like and with whom they can build long-term relationships.

You must connect with people in life and business to be successful. You must talk to people over the phone to sell them your products – and that goes even for the greatest marketing companies in the world. Eventually, your 'abandoned cart' must mean enough to you to provide an additional option for prospects: talking to them.

You must meet people face to face to sell, and build up rapport and long-standing relationships that last.

KEY POINT

Humans buy from humans they like or look like, and with whom they can build relationships.

The more you connect the more you collect

You must connect with people: smile at each other, look each other in the face, shake hands, question, communicate and talk to all your clients personally, like you would with your family. This is more achievable now than ever before, involving video, Facebook lives, conferences, travelling and finding out where your customers are.

One of my Elite Closing Academy members said to me recently:

> *My problem is, I just don't seem to get enough leads through Facebook, LinkedIn and email. My pipeline is empty and I'm sick of being told about this marketing system, that lead generator, this funnel...*

Do you know the feeling?

My solution asks Hard High-Quality Questions. My first question to this Elite Closing Academy member was: 'Where would your ideal customer gather in groups?'

> Member: *Easy, in shopping centres. My perfect customers are shoppers.*
>
> Me: *Where is your nearest shopping centre?*
>
> Member: *Our town centre.*
>
> Me: *What are you doing this Saturday?*
>
> Member: *No idea, why?*
>
> Me: *Go down there and set up a pop-up showroom, make great eye contact with people. Have an awesome Prospecting Pain Question (P.P.Q.) ready to ask that initiates a response, and where relevant, a meaningful conversation.*

The results of doing that – meeting prospects face to face where they gather – were powerful. Lots of leads, follow-ups, data-sharing, information-gathering and some sales for those that needed the product right now.

To connect with other humans, you need to have some basic knowledge of how amazing we actually are. The results might surprise you.

The handshake

A really powerful example of this is when you meet someone for the first time and shake their hand. There are three types of handshake to look out for:

1. Limp-wristed, with poor grip and poor eye contact.

2. An uncomfortably over-the-top squeeze, with too much eye contact. The Romans called this 'the upper hand'.

3. The perfect flat palm to flat palm: same pressure, done with a natural, friendly energy.

Remember: your body language is a reflection of what is going on inside.

Take a moment to think about the last time you met someone with a limp-wristed handshake. What were your immediate thoughts?

- Did you like them?

- Could you trust them?

- What were they hiding?

Take a moment to think of the last time you received a call from someone with a quiet, low-energy voice. Were you compelled to have a great conversation with them? Does this sound completely stupid, or does it ring a bell?

I invite you to recall someone you have met or know who shakes your hand aggressively, taking the upper hand and staring you out at the same time, normally with a loud, powerful voice:

- What are they like as a person: soft and friendly, or strong and aggressive?

- Do you like being around them?

- Will you be comfortable being dominated by this person?

Try to recall a phone call when the person came over as loud and aggressive. Did it compel you to listen for long, or were you thinking: '*How do I get this person off the phone now?*' How do you react to an overly pushy salesperson?

Finally, think about how nice it feels when someone you meet shakes your hand cordially, with a friendly smile and applying the same palm pressure as you. It leaves a lasting, warm feeling on your palm, and an even deeper lasting memory in your brain. I call this *Denting*. Leaving a warm emotional memory.

Think of a time you received a nice, friendly, professional phone call that made sense, had a purpose and felt good. How did it end? It feels good doesn't it, the phone equivalent to a nice handshake.

How can we tell so quickly what we are using to make these immediate and instant decisions?

Use your heart for a change

Stop using email to do all your sales communication, and please stop negotiating online. We have the power through Zoom, Skype and video to connect, so we can see and hear our prospects, using our ancient senses and brain.

We are using sight, touch, smell and sound, but mostly we are immediately connecting via the magnetic energy in our hearts. The same connection happens through the tone of your voice on the phone. Get it right and you have a great start. Get it wrong, and the call will go badly.

Your voice was not given to you for you. You don't need a voice. It is a gift given to you so that you can communicate with others who can hear what you think.

We have 40,000 neurons in our hearts that have the same identity as cells in the brain. Our heart has a brain. It has feelings. Our hearts give off and receive electrical pulses and energy. Our heart can connect with others before we think. Our feelings are connected to our tone of voice. Our brains are connected to our palms, which are connected to our ancient brain: some call it our 'gut' feeling.

We have thousands of times more magnetism in our hearts than anywhere else in our body. We use it to fall in love, feel happy, buy, sell, be compassionate and decide what we do and don't like. It must not be underestimated.

KEY POINT

Let your heart do the thinking.

We use our gut feeling all the time to decide if we like people, situations, places, smells, sounds, visions, you name it – our ancient brain is in constant overdrive to help us make decisions and sense danger before it comes.

Think of a time when you walked into a room and sensed a bad atmosphere. You knew there was something wrong before you had even spoken with anyone or seen anything. You just knew. How?

Think about people who are easy to talk to: what position do they hold their palms in when they are making a point, or discussing something with you? I guarantee that mostly their palms will be facing upwards, suggesting that they are open, no threat to you and prepared to listen. Positioning the palms also alters the voice from a mellow, soft, calm tone to a sharp, pointed tone.

To make this easy to understand, think of the opposite. When you're in a heated argument and shouting, I bet your palm is either facing downwards or you are pointing. You certainly aren't softly suggesting, with your palms facing upwards!

What does any of this have to do with increasing your sales, you may ask? When you first meet a prospect face to face or over the phone, you need to be on your game right from the moment they see or hear you, because this is when we make subconscious decisions about people, using ancient patterns – and they are powerful:

Face to face = 0.25 seconds

Over the phone = 4 seconds

When face to face, all of this happens in a quarter of a second.

Over the phone you have 4 seconds, without a handshake, eye contact or physical contact, for that connection to happen. Within that time the receiver has subconsciously decided via your tonality:

- If you are an authority
- Whether you sound convincing

- What kind of handshake you would have, if you met
- What kind of person you are
- What your face looks like
- If they can trust you
- If they could do business with you

Four seconds over the phone, under one second face to face, and definitely by the handshake.

Before you make a phone call today or agree a Zoom call, Skype meeting or appointment, get yourself into a great state, ready to make an immediate impression. It will be the difference between a sale or not.

People buy from people they like (or look like)

Take the time to appreciate how our ancient brains, thought patterns and processes actually affect our interaction. Knowing the basics and being aware of how human minds make decisions is helpful on your pathway to greatness in sales.

I spend at least 45 minutes every day practising tonality, writing scripts, following YouTube channels, studying world leaders in sales, closing and other areas, role-playing and thinking through overcoming objections – all to prepare for communicating with other humans that day in a proper manner. In my sales training I often share the following story, because it helps us to understand how the ancient patterns in the brain work, and how to overcome them successfully. You must think differently in sales to succeed.

In the Maasai Mara grasslands in Africa, ancient tribes have learned to survive in the toughest conditions. They cohabit the land with some of the most feared predators on the planet: hyenas, leopards, buffalo, elephants and lions. Drought makes their living conditions hard at times, and during the most difficult periods, sourcing meat can be challenging.

Using obvious, transparent and higher-level thinking, the Maasai warriors have learned that they can take meat from the kill of a lion pride, as long as they challenge all the normal behaviour patterns that both they, and a lion, expect to happen. They approach the kill in a purposeful manner by walking confidently as close to each other as possible (making themselves appear to be a bigger mass). Lions are used to every living animal running away from them, so the approaching tribespeople cause real confusion in the lions' brains. Onwards they march until the lions run away from the meat – the complete opposite to their powerful instinct. The warriors split up: two stand guard, while one butchers a quarter of the meat before casually throwing it over their shoulder and walking off at the same pace as they arrived. By the time the lions have worked out what has happened, the tribespeople are long since gone, and the pride returns to feed.

Like the tribe's strategy to get meat, my OWAC technique challenges all the normal patterns. It uses a mindset of thinking differently, asking tough questions, just like the tribespeople must have done during the drought when needing food to survive, noticing the obvious by listening to answers, and using great skill to achieve the desired outcome.

Challenging these ancient patterns in our brains around selling and being sold to is the obvious starting place to get better results. Once mastered, overcoming standard stalls such as: 'Call me back, I'm busy', 'I'm interested but send me it all on an email', 'I need to check with my business partners' or 'I want to go ahead, but I'm not ready' becomes a lot easier to understand and therefore overcome.

My training teaches how to overcome these stalls through total transparency and communicating in a completely different way to everyone else in sales, while achieving nuclear results. More importantly, by using our ancient skills of touch, sight, sound, smell and noise as our biggest tools.

3
The Ancient Brain

When it comes to selling and being sold to, let's imagine that our brains are split into three sections. Our communication engages different parts of the brain in a sales situation. We have a 'funnel of fear' designed to protect us by noticing conscious and unconscious threat, which runs from our top to our tail, starting in the cranium and ending in our soul.

Brain 1: the ancient brain

This has just one job: to keep you safe. 'Yes' and 'No' live here. Fight or flight. Fear lives here. If this brain were a colour, it would be black and white. 'Yes, but...' also lives here (look out for this, as it's code for 'I don't trust you yet').

Brain 2: the data brain

This is where numbers, return on investment, times, distances, names, addresses, 'what ifs', possible risks, obstacles or implications and every minutiae of logical information are stored. If it were a colour, it would be grey. If it were an object, it would be like a huge concrete city, with files to store information in the streets.

Brain 3: the emotional brain

This is where creative thoughts live. The future, even though it's not real, lives here. You can use your memory and recall anything, fire up your imagination and think like a child again. If it were a colour, it would be a vibrant green. If it were a place, it would be the colourful, jungle forest with lots of living things, a party with jelly and ice cream, and lots of laughing and fun and £50 notes falling from the sky!

My studies have taken more than twenty-five years for me to fully understand this amazing aspect of human behaviour. Whenever I teach it at my training, on stage, coaching a private client or in groups, by sharing experiences and being in a classroom, my understanding deepens. When live role-playing, I am able to demonstrate the language patterns that trigger our answers and behaviours.

The language we use fires up different parts of our brains. It's crucial that you know how to bypass the part where negative responses and fear live, and get into the two parts of the brain where data and creativity live.

KEY POINT

Bypass fear and negativity by speaking to the right parts of the brain.

The knowledge in this chapter is life-changing for salespeople. For those who don't understand this, here is an example of what they face on a daily basis when having conversion conversations:

We would love to go ahead, but we need to double check the dates and get back to you.

Honestly, I love it, but can you just email the proposal again and ring me in a month?

I've been busy, email me and I will take a look.

It's just not the right time for us now.

I just need to check with my partner, because I promised I wouldn't spend without their agreement.

Not right now.

I think we're away, I will need to check my diary and let you know.

I'm busy, can you call back later?

We just can't afford it right now.

I haven't got the time.

I don't have enough information.

The biggest skill is to ensure that you don't ask closed questions that bring 'No' into play, therefore triggering a Brain 1: yes/no response. The key words to avoid are:

- Are

- If

- Can

- Would

- Should

Let's look at some examples.

Are you interested in getting started? Yes/No

If I can show you a way of saving money right now, would you go ahead? Yes/No

Can I suggest we get this signed today? Yes/No

Would you like to sign this and make payment? Yes/No

Should I go ahead and get the paperwork ready? Yes/No

Questions that start with any of the above (these are just the main culprits, but there are more) will sometimes get a 'Yes', but mainly will get:

We would love to go ahead, but can you email me as I need to think about it.

I describe this as a 'Yes, but'. Or a Brain 1 answer.

What should you replace the words above with? And which part of the brain will you fire up by doing so?

How to bypass the fearful brain

The six words that you need to use to bypass the ancient, fearful part of the brain, that dwells in Brains 2 and 3, are the 5Ws and 1H:

- Who
- What
- When
- Where
- Which
- How

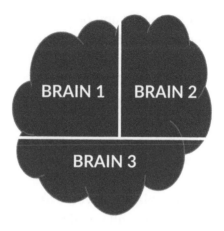

The Three Brains

THE THREE BRAINS EXERCISE

A great exercise I teach all my students is to play around with the words and put one of the 5Ws and 1H words in front of the 'Don't use' words above, to test how easy it is to bypass fear (Brain 1). Go ahead and try it now.

See how the answers to questions that start with 'the don'ts' bring 'No' into play, and how exactly the same questions that start with the 5Ws and 1H open up different parts of the brain and get your prospect's brain thinking for itself.

Close Yourself Cycle

This is powerful when finding out information from a prospect, because it allows them to come up with answers that help you with your outcome. It's even more powerful when closing, because it solidifies the Close Yourself Cycle by enabling your prospect to come to the conclusion that your products or services are the solution they have been looking for, rather than you as the salesperson desperately trying to persuade them to accept it.

Using these techniques in an instinctive way allows you and your team to gather information and qualify the perfect prospect every time you have a conversation, whether that is via email, Messenger, text, Zoom, Skype or other form of communication. It creates a 'towards you' environment that drives an arrow *towards* the truth that lies inside your prospect, along with the solution.

4
Hard High-Quality Questions

Now that you have been introduced to the 5Ws and 1H (a core Elite Closing Academy language philosophy), we are almost ready to delve into the twelve steps.

Just before we do, this is a quick reminder of my belief that selling equals *asking*, not telling. Hard High-Quality Questions are crucial at all stages of sales interactions. Most unsuccessful salespeople and sales teams ask lots of 'closed' questions. These types of questions slowly creep into teams that lack confidence, the skills needed to sell – and, most importantly, it reflects a closed mindset.

These are **the most common closed questions:**

Would you like me to get the sums drawn up?

Are you ready to sign the paperwork?

Can I make an appointment to see you next week?

Is it something you're looking at now?

Would you like to buy one?

Would you like to see my presentation?

Could I interest you in...?

Is there something I could do to change your mind?

Would you like...?

Could I interest you in...?

Do you know your budget?

As you now know, these all fire up the protective part of the brain (Brain 1) and eventually will lead to a slow death in your sales.

Initially, when leads are hot, closed questions may work (these are the 'low-hanging fruit'), but Brain 1 will always take the easy option if it can, particularly when being asked to part with money over the phone, face to face or given a challenging question around a problem or pain that it is experiencing.

Note: your powerful question could be the first time that your prospect is answering a difficult subconscious issue, so please expect some protected answers to these tough questions. Be aware that often, humans will lie about tough, underlying issues they are experiencing in their business – or even within themselves.

Are they telling the truth?

You should be on your guard for what I call 'deferred truth answers', such as:

We were just looking

We're considering it

We're already pretty good at [XYZ] and clicked on your advert because we were just browsing

We have a deep-rooted anxiety of being ripped off, and don't easily share our problems, let alone our credit card details – certainly not to someone we don't like the sound of, or mistrust. When you bring 'No' into play, you decrease your chances of the best outcome straight away.

Ask yourself: how many times have you or one of your staff butchered an opportunity and cost your company money in advertising or marketing by doing this? How many times have you asked yourself or a staff member: 'How did it go with that great lead you were calling today?' only to be told 'We had a great conversation, they're ringing me back tonight at 7 or tomorrow'? – and they never do. Did a closed question give them an easy way out? Has a competitor with better-skilled staff called them since then, and signed them up?

You will never know.

Here are the most common closed questions from above. I have changed the start of them using 5Ws and 1H:

How quickly would you like me to get the sums drawn up?

When are you ready to sign the paperwork?

I would like to make an appointment to present this proposal ASAP. I'm free next Tuesday at 2pm or Wednesday at 3pm – which one suits you best?

When will you be ready to sign?

When would you like to buy one?

How many would you like?

When would you like to see my presentation? I can present this next Wednesday at 2pm or 5pm – which one suits you best?

What could I do to change your mind?

What information do you need from me?

Other than what we have discussed so far, what additional information would your business partner need to read in my email to agree to move forward with us?

By having the problem you just mentioned, what's going to happen if you don't get it solved?

What did you see in me or my product that you believe will help you get a result?

How will we measure the results?

What result are you hoping for?

What's your strongest reason for wanting to change it?

By not solving this now, how long can you carry on?

HARD HIGH-QUALITY QUESTIONS EXERCISE

Try making a situation up and answering both sets of questions (closed and Hard High-Quality Questions) for yourself.

Notice the difference, in particular how your brain works differently when asked Hard High-Quality Questions.

Here are some more Hard High-Quality Questions that are guaranteed to get your potential client thinking about the answers, helping the sales process.

What did you like about our advert?

How can I possibly assist you in making your decision?

What's critical for you to change now in your sales process for closing deals?

On a scale of 0–10 (where 0 is 'terrible' and 10 is 'awesome'), what number would you give yourself?

What's your gap?

What would you like me to put in the email specifically, so that when read, you're compelled to find out more?

How important is this to your business?

When would you like to start?

Remind me, what was your strongest reason for clicking on our advert?

What's your strongest reason for showing an interest in our products?

What do you see in us that you think would help you the most?

We offer places in London or Birmingham. Which one suits you best?

How would you prefer to make the first payment? Mastercard or Visa?

What else can I do now to assist you in taking this amazing opportunity?

Clearly, with so many different industries out there, not all of these questions will be relevant to you.

KEY POINT

Hard High-Quality Questions must start with a who, what, when, where, which or how.

These questions appeal to what Brains 2 and 3 – the parts where the brain must think for itself – must reason and imagine. The left side needs data, numbers, figures and reason, whereas the right side is creative, imaginative and able to visualise the future.

Once it has decided the answer, it memorises that for life – and as long as you have a good experience together, it will always associate your name with the reasons it came up with to use your product, the good experience you had together, and all the other lovely feelings that come with a positive human interaction. Your brain is more powerful than any computer on Earth. Trust it to remember all this. It will.

The brain decides for itself if it wants, needs or likes something. It is your job to ask great questions and allow the process to take place. Powerful stuff.

Try asking great questions in your personal life, it's game-changing. By asking better questions and learning to listen to the actual answer, you will find that both your life and business are enriched unimaginably. Not only will your sales improve, your relationships will too.

5

A Great State

People talk about being in a great state all the time. To be a great salesperson, being in a good state helps enormously. For me, I follow a simple but powerful technique shown to me by Andy Gilbert of Go MAD Thinking called 'Kickstarter' (www.gomadthinking.com).

Each morning I ask myself:

1. What is the single most helpful question I could ask myself for the day?

2. What is a helpful memory from the past to help me for the day?

3. What is the most helpful statement about myself?

4. I visualise the end of the day and all the great things that I have achieved, including the smell, the people I am with, the feelings. What can I see and hear?

This series allows you to focus your brain on clarity, action, techniques and mindset. It also allows your subconscious to have a positive vision of the future, something it needs to succeed.

Bear in mind that the future doesn't exist yet, so it's much more helpful to think like a child and paint a nice, positive picture, rather than allow past or perceived future negativity to shape your action and thinking.

Oxygenate for concentration and focus

A state of concentration

When I'm training people in my sales techniques, I take a few moments to allow plenty of oxygen into my lungs and heart, and allow myself to recall all my learnings that are relevant to the group with whom I'm working. I consider the most helpful question I could ask myself before I start my training.

A state of focus

If I've chosen to do some live phone calls, I again use both oxygen, by moving about the office to create adrenaline, and memory to recall great phone calls from the recent past. Whenever I do live demonstrations on the phone, adrenaline is crucial to me, which is why I nearly always stand up and move about. It enables me to breathe properly and to use my body movements to allow the nuances in tonality and expression to work properly. It is widely believed that when it comes to effective communication, less than 20% of it is down to the actual words, while the rest is made up of body language, tonality and eye contact.

If I'm meeting a client face to face, walking prior to the meeting or at least two minutes of breathing allows me to prepare my mind and make a great first impression. Preparing yourself physically and mentally prior to a meeting, sales call or presentation gets you off to the best possible start. Remember, you literally have a split second to make a good first impression, before the other human both consciously and subconsciously starts to use ancient patterns on you.

GREAT STATE EXERCISE

Write at least one answer to each of the questions below. Feel free to give more answers if they spring to mind. Where it's a quantitative question, score yourself out of 10 (where 10 is 'amazing' and 0 is 'terrible').

If you haven't been preparing yourself up to now, think of the times when you have made a call that turned out badly.

Bad call

- How did the call or meeting start? (0–10)

- How prepared were you? (0–10)

- How much did you actually know about the prospect's pain? (0–10)

- How much did you believe in your product? (0–10)

- What information did you gather about your potential competitors?

- What was your tonality like? (0–10)

- What was your energy like? (0–10)

- What kind of thoughts did you have – hindering or helpful?

- How would you have perceived yourself, had you been the receiver?

- What words did you use at the beginning?

  - *Just a quick call...*

  - *I know you're busy but...*

KEY POINT

Don't use the words 'quick' or 'just' – these activate the ancient, fearful brain.

Think of a call that went really well.

Ask yourself the questions above and see what answers you come up with. I can guarantee that there will always be a difference. I always look for at least an eight out of ten for any of them; anything lower is a signal for immediate review.

Prepare yourself in the best possible way, and you will increase your chances of success.

PART TWO
OPEN WITH A CLOSE

6
Why You Should Open With A Close

I have been using OWAC since I was 18. I remember watching grown adults, sales executives, cough and splutter their way through sales conversations using every old tactic in the book to make it appear that they were not selling something, when in fact they were. And mostly doing it terribly, with poor results. Calls used to start:

I'm not trying to sell you anything, but...

These days, people are sick to the back teeth of long, boring, confusing sales pitches. We just want people to get to the point. We're not stupid, we know you're selling something, so if you just get on with it and the product gets me a result, I might decide to buy it. But please don't take up loads of my time, use aggressive techniques that challenge my right to say 'No', or pretend you're not selling when we all know you are. 'Let's have a chat...', 'Let's touch base...', 'Come to my networking event...', 'Let's get together for coffee...' are all pretences.

It is this belief and understanding that led me to create the OWAC system. It does exactly that:

- Gets to the point through qualification at each and every stage

- Stays on point by demonstrating a reason for the call or meeting for both parties (intention)

- Shows a clear pathway to a mutually beneficial deal for both parties

By qualifying the reason for the call, meeting or presentation, it opens with the outcome of that contact. That way, everyone is aware of exactly what the intentions of the meeting are, and are happy being in truth, ready for your pitch.

KEY POINT

People aren't stupid, so don't treat them like they are. They know you have something to sell, so be totally transparent and set your intention from the beginning.

This is also totally dependent on the salesperson having done the prospecting part of the process extremely well, and been given all the data required to decide:

- The dates and times

- The commitment required

- The price investment

- What is involved to get results and crucially, the real challenges (PUNT with a Q)

- What they need from you to overcome those challenges

- How urgent it is to resolve the challenges, while building massive trust between people

KEY POINT

Remember: businesses are people.

I created this technique after listening to many colleagues use the following kind of lines, and then go on to have ordinary sales calls with ordinary results.

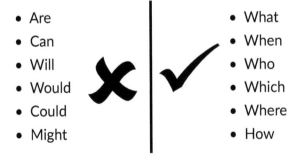

- Are
- Can
- Will
- Would
- Could
- Might

- What
- When
- Who
- Which
- Where
- How

Hi, my name is… I'm not trying to sell you any-thing.

Hi, my name is… we spoke six months ago, and you said to call you back today.

Hi, my name is… so, it's just a quick call to find out if… well, you said to call back… are you interested?

OWAC is the total opposite to everything above. I bet you're dying to know what the twelve steps are.

Open With A Close twelve steps

1. Data means certainty

2. Marketing rapport words

3. Control your thoughts – hindering or helpful

4. Have a desired outcome

5. Certainty checklist

6. The first 4 seconds

7. The Golden Question

8. Power of the pause

9. Close or stall

10. Stall or close

11. The Sixteen-Digit Close

12. Thank you. Who else do you know?

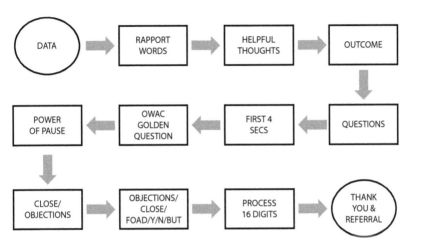

The Open With A Close Process

The result of using OWAC is that the quality and direction of all of your sales conversations at any point of the Prospecting Journey are super-focused, therefore saving time and money.

Open With A Close script in action

In the next sections I'm going to unpack this process and show you a script, and you're going to see how you can use these techniques for your own sales process. The twelve steps are incredibly powerful. Here's an example script for closing a sale over the phone.

Qualification

Hi, is that David?

Yes, David here.

Hi David, it's Matthew... Elite Closing Academy.

Hi Matthew, how are you?

Great, thanks.

Qualified: time to transition to them

David, firstly, thank you so much for the interest you have shown in my two-day training. **(OWAC 2: marketing rapport words)**

The purpose of today's call is to get your place secured at one of my next two events. **(OWAC 4: have a desired outcome)**

We have spaces available on 22 or 23 August, or 26 or 27 September. Which dates work best for you? **(OWAC 7: Golden Question)**

Do not speak! (OWAC 8: power of the pause)

I'd love to come, but I can't make any of those dates. **(OWAC 9: close or stall)**

Use the 3As: agree, appease, accelerate

I appreciate you can't make those dates. **(Agree)**

We also have 24 or 25 October, and 26 or 27 November. **(Appease)**

Which one of those dates would work? **(Accelerate)**

I could do November, so give me a call the last week of October to get me booked on, it's too far away to pay anything now. **(OWAC 10: objection or close)**

Fair point **(Agree)**, *it is a long way off* **(Appease)**, *that's why we split payments into two for you* **(Accelerate)**. *So, you can put £250 plus VAT down today which secures your place and makes sure you don't miss out. We can take the balance of £247 plus VAT on the last week of October.*

What's the sixteen digits across your card, and I will get your spot secured? **(OWAC 11: the Sixteen-Digit Close)**

Oh OK, yes – I will just grab my card.

So, it's [card number], expires [XX/XX], last three digits [XXX], property number [X], postcode [X].

Great, so here's what happens next.

My team will send you an email with all the information that you could possibly need regarding the two-day training in November. Once you have received it, you will also get reminders and any questions you have should be answered. If not, I will personally text you my mobile number, so that you can text me if it's urgent.

Thank you for placing this order, we're really looking forward to seeing you in November. Oh, just before you go – who do you know right now who might possibly need to attend my two-day training? **(OWAC 12: thank you. Who else do you know?)**

This is the perfect time to upsell (more about that another time).

When reading it you can see how the steps work: notice how I stick to the twelve-step process wherever I can. You should also note that I am prepared to come 'offline' but always return to the twelve-step process.

There is a clear start and finish during the call or meeting, and this should happen during every experience. For this script to work, you need to master the twelve steps and repeat.

Real-life example of Open With A Close in action

I have recreated a real-life situation for you here, with tonality details. **See if you can spot the twelve steps of OWAC, the Hard High-Quality Questions, and how I connect to the ancient brain.** Remember, this approach works in all industries, so use your imagination to make the situation relevant to your business right now.

I was working with a company that sold tickets to live events. The tried-and-tested sales strategy involved a massive online marketing campaign to create some real interest in the event being staged to the relevant audience, then following up by getting them onto a priority list by offering their email address and phone number. By being on the priority list, they would ensure receiving the biggest discounted ticket prices, best deals, seat options, etc – a win-win all round.

Many tickets were sold online, but hundreds had 'abandoned cart' after checking out the website. Someone was interested, life got in the way and they failed to purchase a ticket for the event. I devised this script for all those that had not purchased online (command tonality required is shown in brackets, 'D' = down tone):

Hello, is that…? (D)

This is Matthew… [rapport word]… coming up in May. (D)

Firstly, (D) thank you so much for clicking on the link about (rapport word)… and for applying to be on the priority list. (D)

The reason for my call (D) is to make sure (D) that you don't miss out on (D) the amazing (D) discounted ticket price before it goes up next Friday at 5pm.

Which category of tickets would you like? (D)

Access all areas.

Fabulous, great choice. How many seats do you need?

Just one.

Great, normally that would be £1,499 plus VAT and I can get that secured today for just £997 plus VAT (available online also). What's the sixteen digits across your card and I will get that processed for you? (D)

Most people laugh out loud at this point, and pay you a compliment along the lines of: 'You're good!', or 'Wow, that's the best sales call I've had in ages'.

Why do people think this is the best sales call they have ever had? This is because you have:

1. Connected with them by using their name (rapport)

2. Used warm and friendly tonality (ancient brain/ handshake)

3. Engaged their memory by repeating a rapport word (helpful assumption that they are interested)

4. Created some urgency that is of benefit to them (a strong reason to say 'Yes')

5. Used positive language (created warm emotions)

6. Taken the answer 'No' out of play (Hard High-Quality Questions)

I can hear you saying, 'Yes, but this is a really easy qualified lead, a tap-in.' This is true, but you would be amazed at how many 'tap-ins' end up not buying because the caller was in a poor state, got their tonality wrong, used questions that brought 'No' into play, or simply did not follow the system.

Want to see how to get it wrong?

> *I can see you were looking at buying a ticket* (presuming)

> *Would you like a ticket?* (bringing 'No' into play, firing up the ancient fight-or-flight area in the brain, which causes answers such as the following two classics)

> *Yes, but I'm busy – call me back next week.*

> *I just need to think about it.*

KEY POINT

To be really clear, by bringing the option of 'No' into play when closing, you fire up the ancient brain. People will nearly always take the safe option and buy themselves time before purchasing. Your lack of skill at this point creates uncertainty in the buyer, and more often than not they will move away from you.

Sometimes, just sounding like you're reading from a script, being in low energy, getting your tonality wrong, being too weak or too strong and aggressive, or simply sounding too salesy can lose you what should be an easy sale. How many times have you sat in your sales office and heard a colleague try desperately to 'sell' something that should have been an easy 'tap-in'?

The script above was the realistic easy close to a **scorching hot qualified lead.** The challenge is how to overcome the inevitable objections.

Now that you have some of my foundations, it's time to delve deeper into the twelve-step OWAC sales system.

7
Step 1: Data Means Certainty

Before you sell a product or a service, you have to know absolutely every single piece of critical information for one reason and one reason only: *certainty*. In particular, if you have staff, you have to assume that they know nothing about anything, because they will never understand your products and services like you do unless you teach them from scratch. It consumes your time initially, but undoubtedly will prove to be the best investment you have ever made.

A lack of certainty in a salesperson fires up Brain 1, and creates fear and uncertainty in the buyer. It can be as simple as 'I'm not sure – I will ask and get back to you', which can lose you the sale in a hot lead close scenario.

To all you bosses, sales directors or team leaders out there – this, along with a lack of skills, is the number one reason that salespeople fail as new employees. You haven't given them the certainty they need around the business, its purpose, culture, successes, products or services.

KEY POINT

It is your responsibility to make sure that your salespeople are certain about your product.

Most inductions go something like this:

Hey all, this is [X], the new telesales person.

Grab a few brochures and have a read, then go and sit by Tina for an hour – we will have you on the phone by lunch.

That is just not fair, even for a seasoned professional. Giving your employees all the skills and knowledge they need is crucial to achieving quality, long-term results.

Now, as the salesperson you must ensure that you find out the key details of what you will be selling. Here are few of the most obvious:

- **Prices:** including payment plan options, discounts, additional value. We are looking for *what can you do, not what you can't do.*

- **Dates:** includes all future suggested dates and backups to those dates, if they can't attend the original ones given (in the case of events or meetings).

- **Value:** other than money, what value can you offer to get a deal?

- **Terms and conditions:** what are the company T&Cs?

- **Background:** who created the product or service, and what was the purpose of its creation?

- **Problems solved:** what problems does the product or service solve, what are the key benefits?

- **Time:** if it's a course, how long does it last, how much time commitment is there?

- **Details:** if it's a coaching package, how long are the sessions, what happens if the client misses one, what's the refund policy?

You're not looking for a forensic level of detail – in fact, that can get in the way. Just certainty around the product and service.

CERTAINTY EXERCISE

Using the list above, write your own answers for your business, service or product. Then, when you onboard your next salesperson, you'll be ready to get them to certainty fast, and they'll start making a positive impact!

'What if?' destroys confidence

The fact is, salespeople's biggest fears are around the 'what if':

- What if they say 'No'?

- What if they ask me a question and I don't know the answer?

- What if I say the wrong thing?

This is why your induction process should:

- Be purposeful

- Be deep with data

- Involve other departments, such as marketing and accounts

- Allow time to ask questions and read

- Allow time to take simple tests involving the answers that you would expect to give as the owner, director or sales manager, if you were asked

- Include daily role plays and objection handling

- Include regular monitoring and feedback on calls

- Offer a training aspect to enable learning, development and skill growth

Once a salesperson can confidently make calls or speak to a prospect live and from a position of complete and utter certainty around these five points, the results will improve:

1. What result the product gets

2. What pain the product solves

3. Confidence that the product works, with tangible examples

4. A reason why it should happen now, rather than later

5. All the financial opportunities available

Then they will have certainty.

8
Step 2: Marketing Rapport Words

Knowing what word sparks an emotion inside a human's brain and brings them towards your product is extremely helpful:

- What struck a chord with them, and made them believe it was worth their while to find out more and visit your website?

- What made them download some free content, and click on the free training that triggered a call?

- What words encouraged them to book a free consultation, and agree to go on an email list to receive offers or a landing page to get the best deals?

- What emotion led them to attend a webinar, buy a book, or join your free community as the first part of your business funnel?

KEY POINT

At some point the prospect, be it a person or a business owner, has seen something in your products or services that they need or want.

Speak to the marketer to find out what the key words were that they used in the email campaign, book or Facebook advert to attract prospects.

Taking the example used earlier in the book about one of my clients who runs live events, their main marketing words are around growing five, six and seven-figure businesses to the next level. The key word is 'growth'. The truth is that the opposite of growth – stagnation or flat lining, both *red word language* – is what they were most likely experiencing in business that made them click on the *green word* – growth. Does this make sense? Go back and have a look at the red and green words in Chapter 1 if you need a refresher.

Understanding the simple example above – that the key word is 'growth' – creates a powerful undercurrent in your mind that the person who has come towards you via the marketing (in this case) wants or needs to grow their business. For example, it's helpful to presume that your 'Twelve Months Grow Your Business Mentoring Package' is going to:

1. Get them a result

2. Solve problems they have

It's now so much easier to ask a question such as:

> *Thanks so much for clicking on the link. What is it about our mentoring package that you feel would help your business growth over the coming twelve months?*

Or:

> *Thanks so much for clicking on the link. What was the one key word that resonated with you the most? And how do you think that would help your business grow?*

When you know the marketing rapport words, it helps you ask powerful questions that are linked to your outcome of doing business together at some point in the near future. It also enables you to control the conversation, knowing that they have some kind of need or pain.

RED AND GREEN WORDS EXERCISE

Make a list of the red and green words for your service or product.

It is OK to presume at this point that they need what you do.

9

Step 3: Control Your Thoughts – Hindering Or Helpful

When you are across steps 1 and 2 of the OWAC system, all of the data about the product or service that's on offer, and understand the most likely reasons why the prospect has come towards your message, you get clarity. When you have total clarity then it is your job, *your responsibility*, to assist the prospect in the logical next step and give them the solution to the problem.

Your personal mindset will massively affect both your own and your team's outcomes. Be in a helpful mindset, and watch the results.

Having all the data (OWAC step 1), knowing what words spark enough emotion for the prospect to take action and find out more (OWAC step 2), all lead to you and your team easily replacing the natural negative chatter that goes on in the brain with helpful thoughts, so you can get on with making the calls, locking down presentations, setting up appointments, going to face-to-face meetings – whatever the logical next step is.

Over the last twenty-three years, I have worked with sales teams all over Britain, Europe and America. The first thing I do when introduced to a new team is listen. What I'm really looking for is if they are on the phones, hard. Then I look for great use of language, both body and verbal. Remember, your body language reflects how you feel inside.

All good teams share some striking similarities:

- Nearly all shake hands well

- They always make great eye contact

- They always ask great questions that start with: Who, What, When, Where, Which or How

- They listen more than they speak

- They challenge ideas through discussions and questioning

- They are on time

- They are happy to work late

- Their meetings are short and interactive, with clear outcomes and actions

- When they talk, they generally use palms up, open body language

- They are open and frank about results, techniques and data

- They are always happy to share opinions, good practice and help others

- They are happy to do live role play and demonstrate techniques

- They dress smartly

- They smile and laugh a lot

Stale or stuck teams differ in all these areas. They tend to use a lot of general assumptions and presumptions such as:

No one is buying in our industry at the moment.

Everyone doesn't have the money at the moment.

This is negative thinking and totally untrue, unless of course they have lined up every human in the industry that they are referring to, and asked to see a copy of their personal finances and access to funding options!

Here are some common words and phrases to look out for in trapped sales minds:

It's not my job.

Someone else is responsible.

'Can't', 'haven't', 'might', 'try', 'if', 'but', 'couldn't', 'won't'…

Maybe next week…

Haven't got the time…

These are some of the most common phrases I hear from stale or stuck salespeople:

There's no point ringing them now, they will be busy.

We tried that before and it doesn't work.

Let's do it the same as always.

I've been doing this for thirty years, there's nothing I don't know that you could teach me.

Lunchtime's never a good time.

I spoke to them six months ago and they weren't really interested then.

They won't pick up now.

They said they needed to think about it for a bit.

They said they really wanted to do it, but it's not the right time.

They're going to have a chat with their partner and call us back.

I'm sending them an email now.

I was late this morning because the roads were busy again.

I didn't have time to eat breakfast, so I'm just going to the shops.

I don't like doing role plays.

Everyone I've tried to ring just isn't interested.

This is where 'hindering thoughts' live.

KEY POINT

Here's the great news – hindering thoughts can be easily replaced with more helpful thoughts by choosing yourself.

Replace hindering thoughts

Here are a few examples:

By answering the phone, they are proving that they are interested.

Now is a good time to call.

Having thought through our amazing offer, they are ready to buy and will say 'Yes' when I ask the question.

They cannot live without our services – since the last time we spoke, things have got worse for them and now is the perfect time.

To be clear, having a few hindering thoughts and doubts is perfectly normal and reasonable. Sometimes, knowing what didn't work is helpful.

Have your staff ever complained about trying something new? Ever heard about all the things that went wrong last time? We know what didn't work, so what possible lessons can we learn this time to make sure it does work?

Does it sound too simple? Well, our brain is so powerful that if you allow it to visualise positive outcomes, see the opportunities and brilliant end results, it fires up the subconscious brain, which then works tirelessly to get to the outcome. One of its only limitations is not being able to tell if a dream is real or not.

Think about it. Have you ever experienced a nightmare and woke up out of breath and sweating? That was you physically living a dream. The brain can't differentiate, so your dreams in business, sales outcomes and thought processes have to be as positive as possible to allow the brain to create a pathway to reality.

Creating an environment and culture in your business where it's easier to see all the reasons why we should call someone or set up a meeting, as opposed to why we shouldn't, will have a dramatic effect on results.

KEY POINT

It is easier to think of all the reasons why your product is perfect for a potential customer than why they wouldn't want it!

Therefore, team meetings that are open and honest with an outcome, followed by action, will always help provide this culture.

I'm giving you two exercises in this chapter, because getting your mindset right is so important.

TEAM MEETING EXERCISE

In your next team meeting, focus on asking great questions such as:

- What went well?
- What can we learn?
- How could we possibly develop?
- What can we do even better next time?

Ask your team to:

- Share positive thought trails, visions and outcomes.
- Share their dreams.
- Use their imaginations.
- Share the things that didn't work out.
- Ask: what lessons could we learn from this?
- Brainstorm: how could we possibly do it differently next time?

Remind them of your company's purpose, its core values, and enable their imagination to see great end results. As previously mentioned, once it's embedded, the brain actively seeks the result.

Ask them to share their feelings and emotions as well:

- When you sold that £25k deal, what kind of rapport did you have with the customer?
- When you upsold that £1k offer, what worked?
- What lessons are there so we can improve even more?
- How did it make you feel?
- How can we all recreate the feeling you just described?

Your individual mindset will massively affect both your own and your team's outcomes. Be in a helpful mindset and watch the results.

THE MAT OF TRUTH EXERCISE

In your next team meeting, put a mat on the floor (or imagine there's a mat there). Each team member in turn will stand on the real or imaginary mat. While they are on the mat they are not allowed to speak, only listen. The rest of the team has to answer these questions about the person on the mat:

1. What is the person on the mat amazing at doing?
2. What could they do more of, or be even better at doing?
3. If they had one area to develop, what would it be?

Give the person 30 seconds to think through what has been said, then they have three options:

1. Select one piece of information and take action on it, without feeding back to the group
2. Ignore everything they have heard
3. Decide what to take action on, and share it with the group

---

This is how we keep working towards a constant search for the truth, with great questions.

It takes a higher level of thinking and attitude to replace hindering thoughts with more helpful ones. As you're finding out in the OWAC process, the way you are thinking determines the result.

10

Step 4: Have A Desired Outcome

There is nothing worse than receiving a call that starts with, 'I'm not trying to sell you something,' or, 'It's just a quick call to tell you that we can help businesses like yours,' or questions that appear to be a friendly customer service call that turn into a sales call.

It's the same as when someone face to face starts with the intention of helping, serving or asking a few questions (as mentioned previously, a coffee meeting or touching base both being code for hard selling), then at the end of what you thought was a prospecting meeting, turns into the salesperson trying to persuade you into buying something that you're just not ready to buy yet.

Think about a time you felt you were being persuaded by a salesperson to buy a product or a service to which you were not emotionally or logically attached. How awkward is it at the end when you're trying to find a polite way of saying 'No'? Responses such as: 'I'm really interested but I just need to check with my partner,' or 'I can see the benefits of working with you right now, but it's just not the right time,' are code for *this doesn't feel good – back off*. It's a bit like going on a first date and going in for the snog before you've even had some popcorn!

Here's another crucial reason why you need to be clear on your outcome: it enables you to stay on track during the conversation and to ask powerful questions that are directly linked to your desired result. It saves time, means you get straight to the point, and allows you both consciously and subconsciously to work towards a future desired outcome in a plain, easy-to-follow way.

What are outcomes, anyway?

When closing a hot, qualified lead there can only be three outcomes:

1. *Yes please, I need your product right now – if I don't have it, something bad will happen to me or my business.*

2. *Yes but…* Almost always at the hot, qualified lead stage, whatever they say after *but* is the reason *why* they should do it.

3. *F**k off and die (FOAD) – it really is not OK right now.* This is unlikely. While it is a truly horrible thing to say to another human being, please remember that it is literally the worst thing that can happen in sales! A 'No, thank you' is *not* going to kill you. Remember: a 'No' is only now, not forever – it is your duty to make sure that it's a 'No' after being armed with every last piece of information.

You have to be comfortable with all three outcomes when closing hot, qualified leads.

Let's look at the best outcome, option 1. Imagine if your partner were to call you, panicking because a wild animal had escaped from the local zoo and was gallivanting about in your back garden. Your elderly mum and dad were looking after your kids at the time, who are only eight and twelve years old.

Here's the good news: grandad was quick and dived into the garden shed, saving the girls from imminent death. But now they are all stuck in there, with a hungry animal salivating on the shed window. Here's the great news: your next-door neighbour has a double-barrelled shotgun. He's a crack shot and has offered to kill the animal, saving your whole family.

The bad news? He wants £50,000 for doing the deed. In cash!

Your mum wants to know what you're going to do? She is screaming at you down the phone! Do you:

1. Say, 'Email me the details and I'll have a look'?

2. Say, 'I just have to check with my partner…'?

3. Find the money, right there and then, to save your family?

Not a difficult question, is it? If you had the money, you would send it over to your neighbour immediately. If you didn't, you would find it – beg, borrow or steal it. Why? Because your family's safety is vitally important to you.

This is the wild animal in the garden moment! When your prospect needs what you are offering, it's the only solution to their problem, and something bad will happen to them if they don't get it.

Quick note: the rules are totally different when prospecting and cold calling, and the possible outcomes are totally different for cold and warm traffic. (I will be discussing this in my next book: *The 4 Steps of the Prospecting Cycle.*)

Even though you want outcome 1, remember that all three outcomes are a good result. Even a FOAD, because at least you will never have to waste your time, energy and money with a business or prospect that doesn't need what you do.

The problem for most salespeople is that they are so afraid of getting outcome 2 ('Yes but...') or outcome 3 (FOAD), that they don't make the calls. Knowing the different nuances and the expected endings helps you get results and keeps you on track during the communication.

KEY POINT

You will have a better chance of getting to outcome 1 if you get to the prospect's critical, real problems fast.

The majority of salespeople don't go to where the real pain is, and that is why they get the 'ring me back' or 'pop me an email' responses. Your solution isn't important enough to the prospect because:

1. You aren't speaking to the right person

2. You haven't found the important, critical problem

Let's do our good news/bad news scenario again.

Consider this. You are on holiday, walking along, minding your own business when suddenly an aeroplane wheel falls out of the sky and lands on you, breaking your leg. You're whipped off to the nearest emergency room. The good news is that there's a brilliant orthopaedic surgeon who tells you that if they operate right away, they can save your leg. Yay! The bad news is that you're going to have to pay for the operation yourself.

The worse news is that if they don't operate right now, not only will you lose your leg, you're going to die! The good news is that if they operate, you'll live and get to play football again. And the great news is it's only going to cost you £125,000 not to die!

What are you going to do? Say, 'Pop it on an email to me, and I'll get back to you'? No! You'll find the money to get what you need because this is a critical, real, urgent pain.

The diagram below is called the 'Christmas Tree', which highlights that if the conversation is getting a little off point (meaning away from one of the expected endings), then you must ask a Hard High-Quality Question linked to the outcome of the call to get back on track.

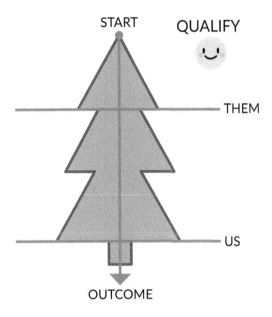

The Christmas Tree Conversation Guide

You will hear me on the phone regularly say (in a qualified hot lead scenario):

> *Mr Smith, I totally understand that you're busy, I will get straight to the point... How many tickets would you like to our event?* (3As technique)

Or:

> *I understand that you need to take more time. Flip back with me: what was it that made you click on the link in the first place?* (Bullseye Flip Back technique)

KEY POINT

Only ever ask questions that are linked to your outcome.

Stop asking questions like:

How's business?

How are things now?

Tell me about your business.

Knowing your desired outcome, your endpoint, focuses the mind: once armed with the skill of asking outcome-linked, Hard High-Quality Questions, the results are unreal. It's called being 'laser-focused': something that is massively sought after as everyone is 'busy'! Time is more valuable than money.

ANIMAL IN THE GARDEN EXERCISE

Take 15 minutes right now and think about your prospect. What's their wild animal in the garden? Ask yourself these questions:

1. What does your prospect need?
2. How are you the solution to their problem?
3. What bad things might happen to them if they don't get what they need from you?

11
Step 5: Certainty Checklist

The question I ask myself before any single sales contact, phone call, live event, face-to-face meeting or group training day is:

> *What would Matthew Elwell need to hear today, from Matthew Elwell, for Matthew Elwell to believe that Matthew Elwell could get Matthew Elwell a result?*

What words would I need to hear to strike a chord in my emotional home, to draw me towards the belief that the product or service on offer would work for me or my business? This is what creates certainty.

If you have done the previous steps right, you will have certainty that:

1. You know that your prospect needs what you do

2. You understand their pain and urgency

3. You have all the data you need to help the client

When you have the internal certainty, nothing can stop you. That is what we are looking at in this chapter.

Reason for calling or presenting

Here is a list of just some of the questions salespeople that are trained by me *ask themselves* prior to going into a contact, so that they can build their certainty:

- What data would I need to decide?

- What emotional connection could we possibly have to assist the sales process?

- What kind of language should I use?

- What will I say if they object or stall?

- What are the likely reasons they wouldn't do it?

- What's the most likely reason they would do it?

- Other than money, what else would they get by working with us?

- Who else might they know that I can use as a reference?

- What other results have we got, either in their industry or with a competitor?

- Who else other than the MAN (Money Authority Need/decision-maker) could possibly influence this decision?

- Who else in the organisation could possibly assist or help me get my message across to the MAN?

- What key rapport words will strike a chord with this person?

- What do I already know that is helpful to us working together?

- What would their strongest reason be for wanting my services?

- What problems will we overcome?

- What results will we get?

- What's the perfect product to get them a result?

- What measurable results would they need to get for it to be the best business investment of all time?

- What else do I know that is helpful?

- Who else could I possibly involve now to assist the contact, eg marketing department, managing director, sales manager?

- What's my state like?

- What data am I not sure about?

- What rapport words are going to be relevant, if needed?

- What's the most helpful thought I could have to assist a great result?

- What's my desired outcome?

Remember: you only have four seconds on the phone call for the other person to judge you. They will be creating a picture in their head, deciding if you are valuable or important to them, if they can trust you and whether you sound professional. It is even quicker in person: as mentioned previously, you get less than a second for them to pick up on your tone of voice, body language, eye contact, proximity, handshake and decide if they want to listen to you. We are going to cover this first 4 seconds more in the next chapter.

KEY POINT

Your voice was not given to you for you; it was given to you for other people.

They will decide whether to listen to you, and if they understand you. You need to practise achieving a great tone of voice, a warm handshake and projecting confident body language. These all get better when you have certainty within.

CERTAINTY CHECKLIST EXERCISE

One of the best ways to get certainty from within is to role play. Find someone you can role play with, and work through your script with them. Get them to ask you questions as if they were a prospect.

Before you start, replace hindering thoughts with helpful ones, make sure your own emotional state is great, and think about your body language. Make sure you are certain about:

- **The data** you have, because data means certainty
- **Your mindset** so you can make an emotional connection
- **Your language,** use rapport words and red and green words
- **Your desired outcome** – ask questions directly linked to your pre-agreed outcome, and never have more than one outcome

These first five steps of the twelve-step OWAC system are all about you and your team. They are to assist you in the contact.

12
Step 6: The First Four Seconds

It is easy to forget just how powerful our brains actually are. We use lots of patterns in language to validate and make sure that we won't be rejected. Salespeople do this all the time.

Hi, is that Mr Smith?

My name is Matthew Elwell, it's just a quick call because the last time we spoke you said to give you a call in six months, so I'm calling today to tell you how we can save you time and money and make you more productive...

That is the kind of language I hear all the time when visiting companies, hearing others and receiving calls myself. Trust me: if you or your staff ever sound like the example above, you're either going to be doing really badly, or run out of leads fast.

When salespeople are doing their job properly, prospects should have your number stored in their smartphone: you should be in their minds, Facebook friends, LinkedIn connections, email communications. You need to be social media friendly with your potential customers. It's the only way.

If you meet someone at an event, a networking meeting or in a bar, don't get their business card; instead, send them a text and get their details on your smartphone straight away, and make sure they save your details. Then text them within 60 seconds of the end of your initial meeting with a free training, or some information in return for their details.

KEY POINT

Make it personal.

When you call someone, say their name:

> *Is that David?*
>
> *Yes.*
>
> *It's Matthew… Elite Closing Academy.*

You will know within a split second, by listening, if they connect emotional thoughts and previous decisions they have made about you, your products and services instantly. Make sure you're listening:

Oh yes, Matthew, great thanks. How are you?

Fabulous, thanks for taking the call. The specific reason I've called is…

Link this statement to your desired outcome, which will differ depending on what stage of the sales cycle your prospect is at: cold, warm or hot. What happens if they don't recall who you are? This creates an opportunity to remind them:

It's Matthew, Elite Closing Academy, calling about my two-day sales training in March.

Tonality must go up, to fire up the recollection area in the prospect's brain. Try it!

Oh yes, I remember – you emailed me last week. Great, how can I help?

That first four seconds is designed to create a smiley face inside before you crack on with your purpose and intention for calling.

THE FIRST FOUR SECONDS EXERCISE

The best way to work on your first four seconds is to role play. Practise your tonality by recording yourself speaking. Try using rising (recollection and question) and downward (command) tones. Deepen your voice. Slow down and speed up. Stand up and speak, sit down. Then listen to yourself.

- How did that make you feel?
- Did you sound confident, rushed, excited or boring?
- What can you do differently?

13

Step 7: Open With A Close Golden Questions

The OWAC Golden Question must be linked to your desired outcome, which we covered in step 4. This is a short chapter but make no mistake, it's also one of the most important. As with most really important things in life, clarity, simplicity and the blinking obvious are true.

If you're having problems with selling, be honest and answer this: how many times do you ask a Golden Question?

What's a Golden Question, I hear you say?

Come on, you know the moment I'm referring to: that bit in the sales call when your heart starts to pump a little bit harder and you have covered all bases, but you just need to ask the obvious question.

It cannot – I repeat, cannot – bring 'No' into play.

The first Golden Question comes right at the end of the first sentence, during the qualifying part of the call.

> *Firstly, thank you for agreeing to today's call.*
> *The purpose of the call is to find out…* **(Golden Question)**
>
> *How many tickets you wanted?*
>
> *When you would like to get started on my mentoring programme?*
>
> *Which date you wanted to get your consult booked in: Friday the 1st or Monday the 4th – which one works for you?*
>
> *Who do I need to send the invoice to for payment?*

These are tried-and-tested techniques which, when repeated with command tonality, guarantee an immediate increase in conversions for one big reason: you are eliminating Brain 1 thinking in your prospect – which the brain will strongly consider taking, whenever it goes straight into protective mode.

KEY POINT

Eliminate the possibility of Brain 1 thinking.

You see, here's the power: by bringing 'No' into play at the moment when the close should be effortless and without doubt, the prospect's subconscious mind picks up on a slight lack of certainty in your language that fires up the ancient last line of defence that they have… gut feeling/funnel of fear.

Our belief is that by giving the prospect the option at this point, it's the opposite of pushy. The converse is true: it creates uncertainty, emotionally and spiritually. Often, this uncertainty leads to:

We're ready to go ahead, but we just need to run the numbers.

Or:

Email me again and I will think about it.

In a hot, qualified lead, it sounds something like:

Hi, is that Mrs Smith?

Yes, Mrs Smith speaking, who's this?

It's Matthew, Elite Closing Academy.

Oh yes, I've been expecting your call.

Great, thanks so much for clicking on the offer page for our next event. The purpose of my call is to get your ticket booked. Which category did you want access to: all areas, or general seating? **(Golden Question)**

You will notice how I use the 4Cs in my language when asking great questions. A salesperson must be:

1. Clear

2. Crisp

3. Concise

4. Certain

Also notice the lack of chit-chat: *What's the weather like, it's just a quick call, I'm not trying to sell you anything, just quickly wondered if...*

All the phrases highlighted above fire up Brain 1 – the feeling that you're about to be sold to.

KEY POINT

Remember, you have already gained massive trust in your prospecting process, and earned the right to ask a closing question.

GOLDEN QUESTION EXERCISE

Ask yourself or your team: 'What Golden Questions do we ask?' When you are asking them in the conversation, remember that they may change, depending on the product or service.

Ask the Golden Question at every opportunity. If you don't, a competitor will.

14
Step 8: Power Of The Pause

When you don't speak in a conversation, you're in control more than you could ever imagine, particularly after asking a Golden Question. When the prospect is choosing, you're in control. The temptation is to ask a question and then continue, using 'leading' language. This causes the prospect to refrain from deep thinking and gives them an easy shortcut to an answer that you want to hear, but does nothing to move the situation along the pipeline.

Here's an example of the wrong way to do it:

> So, I suppose the big question is: what do you like about my product? Was it that you can save money, or that it saves you time?

Time.

Great, thanks.

The best way is to ask:

> *What is it that you see in me and my product that*
> *you believe will get you to an even better result, or*
> *solve a problem that you have with 'closing' deals?*

**Silence. Refrain from asking anything at this point:
do not lead, do not speak – even if there is total
silence.**

When you ask a powerful question, give the prospect
the time and space to consider their answer. Be comfortable with pauses and silences. At my training centre I personally demonstrate this, using the physical
technique of asking a Hard High-Quality Question,
followed by putting both hands over my mouth to
stop myself speaking until I have heard the answer.
It's liberating.

The same technique of silence and pausing must be
used after asking your opening problem question
when cold calling, your opening possibility question
when prospecting (P.P.Q), and when asking your closing questions when closing, eg:

> Cold: *if it were free to work with me for 5 minutes,*
> *what's the biggest challenge when closing sales*
> *right now?*

Warm: *what is it about our product or service that, when implemented in your business, would get you an even better result or solve a problem right now?*

Hot: *what's the sixteen digits across your card, and I will take payment?*

After each one of those questions, it is imperative that you stop speaking and wait for as long as it takes for the answer.

KEY POINT

Wait for as long as it takes, without speaking.

When you ask a world-class question to a world-class human being you get world-class answers – but only when you give them the time and space to answer of their own accord. As salespeople we are so wrapped up in targets, money, numbers and commission that we struggle to ask and *listen*. Great closers ask great questions and listen out for data to help them down the line.

KEY POINT

In negotiation, whoever speaks first after the Golden Question, loses. Don't speak first!

It's a skill that must be mastered. For those that don't ask and listen, opportunities to delve deeper and understand the prospect's needs and pain are missed, leaving you with nothing to hang on to except features, benefit and costs. By asking leading, closed or neutral questions, the road leads to nowhere – both for you and the prospect.

Ask and listen, or ask and stop speaking (fight the urge).

STFU EXERCISE

With a colleague, get into a role-playing scenario. Ask your role-playing partner a Golden Question, such as:

Which date, Friday the 1st or Monday the 4th, works best for you?

Or:

There's two ways to make payment: instalments, which saves you £1,000, or the pay-in-full option, which saves an amazing £2,000. Which one suits you best?

Then put your hand over your mouth and STFU. Do not speak. Say nothing.

15
Step 9: Close And Stalls

We are now entering the final part of this hot, qualified lead script: the closing, where there needs to be a clear change in language after identifying stalls and overcoming them. The big technique that I teach to overcome what most people call objections, although mostly they are trying to delay (delays or stalls), is called the 3As.

First, let's look at what objections really are.

Objections: stalls

The first skill is to recognise the difference between a genuine objection and someone who is buying themselves time to think or just slip away. When someone tells you their objection, it's important to listen. The initial objection is nearly always a gateway to finding out the real reason they are objecting. It is also often the strongest reason why they should buy your product:

I just can't justify spending that now.

Or:

I can see the value, but just can't afford it right now.

Or:

I can't find the time, I'm really busy.

To make this clearer, let's go back to the example we started with earlier.

We are trying to sell tickets to a live event. The prospect from your existing database or online campaign clicked on some marketing, and eventually clicked through both first and second pages. It is fair to presume that they are a warm lead, and have an interest in what you do (in the same way that if you walk into a car showroom, it is fair to presume that you are considering purchasing a new vehicle at some point soon).

There are only three types of lead, although there are nuances (as in brackets):

1. Cold (ice, freezing)

2. Warm (prospect, PUNT with a Q)

3. Hot (hot, qualified lead, green light)

Remember, there are only three types of outcome from a hot, qualified lead:

1. 'Yes.'

2. 'Yes, but...' (Follow the lock down system, *do not* use persuasion at this point – we don't want to force anyone. If they are a problem now, they will be an even bigger problem later, if forced.)

3. 'FOAD' – maybe is not an option.

We have got to the first of our Golden Questions, and this is what the call looks like:

Hi, is that [name]?

It's [name, company].

Firstly, thank you so much for... The purpose of today's call is... How many tickets would you like for the event? **[Golden Question]**

Silence.

The prospect normally laughs out loud at this point, as they just cannot believe that you have got straight to the point and asked them the Golden Question. Remember: they have already had all the details, prices, dates, etc previously.

Remind me, what was the event again?

This is a standard answer to buy them time to think how they could possibly get out of your proposal.

The [X] event in June, in London.

Use words that they were likely to have read in the marketing campaign – marketing rapport words.

Oh yes, I remember.

At this point the person is now totally qualified, and **your reason for calling is totally clear.**

Also, it's the time that the first bank of objections will come your way.

Here are the most common:

I'm busy.

I think I'm on holiday that week, I will have to check and let you know.

I don't know enough about it.

I can't afford it.

I just haven't got the time right now.

Yes I am, but can you email me?

None of the above are actual honest objections in a hot, qualified lead, they are more like stalls because although they may need to check their diary, they still have the problem that made them click the link or show interest in the first place.

Let me ask you a question right now. What was the date of your last holiday? I'm convinced you will remember it quite easily. Let me ask you another question: what is the date of your next holiday? I guarantee that you know the date!

KEY POINT

I always aim to ask closing questions twice while staying on track, before flipping back if they are stalling at this point.

My technique here is called the 3As.

The 3As (when closing)

This technique can be used all the way through the Prospecting Journey, and only differs around *appease* and *accelerate*.

This is an art. It takes training, practice, perseverance, skill and techniques that involve saying things differently to everyone else. After all, Albert Einstein's definition of madness is doing the same things over and over again and expecting different results.

- Rule number 1 of selling globally: always agree. The customer is always right. **[Agree]**

- Then, find a solution or soften things a little. **[Appease]**

- Ask a question to get back on track with your desired outcome. **[Accelerate]**

You have to be able to link any questions you ask to the outcome promptly.

Here are some basic examples:

I'm busy at the moment.

Of course – you're busy, so I will keep this brief. How many tickets to our event would you like?

I just can't afford it.

I appreciate you can't afford it. That's what we will teach you at the event, so let's get you booked onto our most affordable bracket. It's normally £299, but today it's only £199. What's the sixteen digits across your card, and I will secure your space?

The 3As is a powerful technique I teach in my training. As is the Bullseye technique (which I share later). These two techniques alone will enable you to close any product, anytime, anywhere.

KEY POINT

Your language needs to be crisp, clear, concise and certain when closing (the 4Cs).

Here is another great example:

> *Thanks for sharing those concerns. Here's the great news: at our event we will show you exactly what you've just talked about... and... What's the sixteen digits across your card, and we can get you booked on?*

This part of the call is also where one of my most effective live training methods happens: the 3Ps (see below). I spend so much time on this at my training and in the academy, because when mastered the results are huge. However, when done badly, the prospect seems to constantly slip away only, for another lukewarm date in the future to be agreed.

You're on the call to close this hot lead. At this point the prospect is pre-qualified, knows who you are and the purpose of the call. The Golden Question – how many tickets are wanted – has been delivered and you have paused, awaiting the answer. At this point you either get:

Yes, I would like two VIP tickets please.

Or, you get bank number 1 (Bank of Bullshit) which I have set out earlier.

Using the 3As and the Flip Back and Bullseye techniques (which we cover next), it is your job to agree, appease and accelerate back into the close by handling the stalls one by one, and reminding the prospect of the reason they believe they should attend.

The 3Ps

These 3Ps are what build a great attitude and mindset.

PURPOSEFUL

The 3Ps

Purposeful

This is your intention, your desired outcome. I never have a sales conversation with someone I can't help. Cut them loose, be honest and tell them you can't help them. You can only be honest if you have a plan, a purpose for the sales call and know your own purpose.

Professional

You become professional by:

- Having the right tools and techniques

- Knowing your data

- Being able to build rapport

- Being in control of your thoughts

- Being clear on your outcome

Even if a prospect is being a jerk, you stay professional. Professionalism equals transparency. Make your purpose clear at the start of the call: 'The purpose of this call is to do business together...'

Professional also means you are always on time, ring people back and do what you say you'll do.

Persistent

About 85% of emails don't get read properly or even delivered, so be persistent. Send them an email, and a message or text with 'Let me know you got it with a thumbs up,' and try a test close, 'How soon do you want to get started?'

Remember: it takes between five and twelve contacts on average to close a sale. My figures show that only 48% of businesses follow up, and 52% don't follow up at all! Only about 25% follow up three times. Make sure you're not in these stats.

KEY POINT

They haven't gone quiet on you; you've gone quiet on them!

Of salespeople, 90% don't have this purposeful, professional and persistent attitude. They won't go the extra mile. A 'No' might be a no for now, so the way you handle this is critical: you leave an emotional footprint on your prospects. Thank them, then ask:

1. When shall I contact you in the future, or not at all?

2. When we do speak next time, what question should I ask to make us relevant?

3. Who else do you know who might need what we do now?

THE 3AS EXERCISE

Think of a recent call you made that didn't go so well. Write down the progression. Work out how you could have used the 3As to make the call better:

- How could you have **agreed, when they stalled?**
- What words would have **appeased?**
- What question could you have asked to get back on track with your desired outcome and **accelerate?**

Next time you will be better prepared!

16

Step 10: Stall Or Close

Now we can repeat as in the previous step, but deal with the second bank of stalls before returning to the close using the 3As.

These days it has become acceptable to lie to people who call you up. Feel a bit uneasy? When was the last time you answered your phone to a salesperson and said straight away: 'What's this about, I'm busy?'

How can you possibly be busy if you're answering your phone? I'm in the middle of something! Really, well it can't be that important because you have just answered your phone. In fact, the truth is, the only thing that they are busy doing is answering the phone to you and quickly thinking of a simple easy stall to buy themselves more time. If you're swimming in the sea, do you answer your phone? No. You're busy swimming in the sea and your phone has been left somewhere securely.

To be clear, if someone answers the phone and they are genuinely busy, their tonality will make it super clear, very quickly, that they *really are* in the middle of something. That is the time to say – I can hear you're busy, speak later and end it immediately. Please remember to follow the 60-second rule though, and text them straight away!

Here are some regular stalls at the second Bank of Bullshit:

Yes, you just need to email me all the details.

I have got to speak to someone else.

I'm not sure it's the right thing.

What guarantees can you give?

How will I know it will work?

Not one of the above is an actual objection to not attending the event. They are all ways to avoid being sold to and get you off the line. It's your job to learn to tell the difference between genuine objections and standard stalls and deflections.

Once you learn this skill, the results are truly incredible.

Bullseye: Flip Back (when closing)

This example is after the prospect has stalled twice with bank 1 and bank 2, and this is your best option to get the prospect back on track.

The Bullseye technique can be used at any time during the sales process. In a closing situation, we teach you this technique after the first two stalls or objections. This is a simple process to follow in the heat of the battle so that you don't miss the bleeding obvious, and stops the need to think ahead.

Here's an example:

> *I would absolutely love to go ahead, but we're not sure it will get the result.*
>
> *Totally appreciate that.* **[Agree]**
>
> *Results are crucial to us.* **[Appease]**
>
> *What result would you need for this to be the greatest investment you've ever made?* **[Accelerate using Bullseye]**

Answer from prospect:

> *We would need at least five new sales a month.*
>
> Your answer (if it is achievable):
>
> *Perfect, let's get you booked in for your consult. We've got… or… which one suits you best?*

Transition back to the close.

KEY POINT

Maintain your professionalism and be persistent.

You have earned the right to be closing by using the PUNT with a Q system we covered – Pain, Urgency, Need and Trust – so don't let them go. They are just letting their fear of being duped or hard sold to put them off. Elite closers expect this.

I remember I called a woman who had clicked on a link on our website. The conversation went like this:

Hi, is that Jane?

Yes, Jane here.

Hi Jane, it's Matthew… Elite Closing Academy.

Hi Matthew, I'm just jumping into a taxi, I can't speak right now.

Jane, I understand that you're just jumping into a taxi. While I've got you, let me ask you: what made you click on the link on our website?

Jane explained for about two minutes that she was having problems in her business, then she said:

I've got to go, I've got a taxi waiting.

*I understand you've got a taxi waiting. Tell me,
how critical is it to solve your problem?*

Jane spoke for another three and a half minutes, then
said:

I've got to go, the taxi is here.

*I understand that your taxi is there. While I've got
you, what's going to happen if you don't handle
your problem?*

Four minutes later Jane had told me all the pain she
was having, then she said:

What's the next step?

Other salespeople might have just said, 'No problem,
I'll call you back next week.' They wouldn't have
closed the logical next step and she would not have
been served.

BULLSEYE EXERCISE

A great way to practise the Bullseye technique is to:

1. Ask yourself what you hear the most in terms of
   being pushed away during the close.
2. Write down the three top reasons people normally
   give you for not going ahead. For example: 'I would
   love to go ahead, but need to speak to my partner...'

3. Focus on the positive word or one of the last three words spoken and then flip back or repeat. Write down your three responses to the pushbacks. For example: 'When you say you'd love to go ahead, what do you mean?'

17

Step 11: Exchanging Money And The Sixteen-Digit Close

About 40% of people reading this will get stuck at this late stage and not get the payment. That means it's quite likely that you're one of the people who don't get the job done when it comes to taking the money! It's time to change that.

The most powerful question that a closer has is around payment. There will be the right closing question for you and your industry that results in the exchange of money. You just need to practise and get it right.

There are a few issues you will run into at this stage.

The Sixteen-Digit Close

If it is appropriate for your industry and the product or service you're selling, then the best close is the Sixteen-Digit Close. Here are a few great examples:

What's the sixteen digits across the card?

How would you prefer to make the initial payment? Visa or Mastercard?

Which option suits you best: pay in full or the payment plan?

So you want to pay in full, great. That's normally £4,995, but you can save £1,000, making it just £3,995. Which card do you prefer to make the payment with?

Once we've got the payment confirmed we will send you an email with all the details of the [X] on [X date], and if you have any questions please let me know via text, WhatsApp, email or just call me on my mobile number.

You might get one of the four responses below.

1. I don't have a credit card.

   I understand you don't have a credit card, so log onto your internet banking app and I will tell you my bank details over the phone. I never email or text them for safety. Once the payment lands, I will confirm that while you're on the phone.

2. I can't pay on my personal card; email and I'll pay on the company card tomorrow.

   Of course you can't pay on your personal card. I'll send you an email with the invoice tomorrow – while I've got you on the phone, what can you pay on your personal card right now to lock down your space, so you don't miss out and we will refund it on receipt tomorrow?

3. I've not got my card on me.

   I understand you haven't got your card on you right now. Where is it? I'll wait while you go and fetch it.

4. Ring me tomorrow.

   Of course I'll ring you tomorrow, so that you don't miss out. What can you give me right now to lock the space down for you?

It's amazing how many people suddenly find their card!

If you don't get the payment (or part payment) on the phone, you will wait for weeks and often never get the payment. Be 3Ps and use the 3As: Agree, Appease, Accelerate to get the payment.

On one of my Elite Closing Academy training days I did a live demonstration of the Sixteen-Digit Close, it went something like this:

Hi, is that Jim?

Yes, Jim here.

Hi Jim, it's Matthew... Elite Closing Academy.

Firstly, thank you so much for this opportunity. The purpose of today's call is to get you booked on the two-day training. We have spaces in July or August. Which date works best?

Hi Matthew, I'm in but I'm driving right now.

Jim, I understand that you're driving, pull over safely, and I'll hang on.

I'm on the main road, I can't pull over.

I understand that you're on the main road, so what's your safest next left turn?

It's coming up.

Great, take your time.

Jim pulled over and I took his credit card details in front of a live audience.

KEY POINT

Employ the 3Ps at all times to exchange money. Do not let the prospect 'sell' to you with standard stalls.

The Exchange of Agreement Close

If you can't take the money, then agree something in writing or sign a contract. This happens a lot for business-to-business sales, where you're entering into an agreement and you probably need to get heads of terms signed. This is the Exchange of Agreement or electronic close.

If you can't get money, get an Exchange of Agreement:

Who's responsible for getting the invoice paid today?

Who do I send the heads of terms to, to get them electronically signed?

What address shall I put on your contract?

What's the best email address to send the contract to, while we're both on the phone? I'll send an electronic link for signing the contract while I wait.

Of course, you should personalise all of these: communicate with your prospects as you would do with your friends.

KEY POINT

You can follow the OWAC system as successfully as possible, but if you screw up here, all your hard work will be wasted.

SIXTEEN-DIGIT CLOSE EXERCISE

The exchange close needs to be done right, so it is worth thinking through how you will respond in advance. Here are a few to get you thinking: select a couple of your favourite ones, and personalise them ready for the close.

What's the sixteen digits across the card?

How would you prefer to make the initial payment? Visa or Mastercard?

Once we've got the payment confirmed we will send you an email with all the details of the [X] on [X date], and if you have any questions please let me know via text, WhatsApp, email or just call me on my mobile number.

Who's responsible for getting the invoice paid today?

Log onto your internet banking app and I will tell you my bank details over the phone. I never email or text them. Once the payment lands, I will confirm while you're on the phone.

18
Step 12: Thank You And Referral

Now is not the time to waffle on or talk shit. You need to focus. Don't chit-chat or veer off on politics, current affairs or religion. That might lead you into trouble and lose you the sale. Be professional, stay professional.

You have three final jobs to do:

1. Thank them for their business

2. Ask for a referral

3. Sell something else (this is beyond the scope of this book)

Thank them

It sounds obvious, but plenty of people forget this common professionalism: just say 'thank you' for their business. Then, outline the next steps:

Here's what's going to happen next. I'll send you an email with all the details and information about what's agreed. If you need anything else, just let the team know. I'll send you a personal text so you have my number. Call me if you need anything.

Use the 4Cs, be:

1. Clear

2. Crisp

3. Concise

4. Certain

KEY POINT

Be grateful, before asking them for a referral.

Who else do you know?

This is an obvious time to ask for a referral or sell something else, but please be warned this can go wrong and has to be delivered politely, almost as a throwaway.

In the academy we teach it like this (focusing on the referral):

Oh, just before you go, who else do you know right now who needs what we do?

You will get one of two answers:

My friend, Matthew.

Perfect! What's his number?

Then you pick up the phone right away and call them, using your referral script. Or:

I do know someone, but I would want to check they are happy to speak to you first.

Of course, I will mention it in the email for you. (Or put it in my text message.) And you can send them a free training so they can check me out (remember to capture data before giving away free training).

Then confirm via text or WhatsApp that you have sent them an email, and ask for a thumbs up, so you know they have received the email. Whatever answer you get, always thank them – then leave them alone. Be polite, don't confront them if they say 'No', just be natural and back off. Don't risk the sale.

KEY POINT

Be polite, always!

Get on the phone to people who you know or have done business with you, and ask them for a referral. People don't make recommendations because it's not important to *them*. But it is important to you – and you can phone them up and ask for a referral!

REFERRAL EXERCISE

Do a little role play with a friend or colleague, and practise asking for a referral. Make it a casual, throwaway line. Practise until it comes naturally to you.

19
Ready To Try It Yourself?

You can use this summary to create your own scripts, specific to you and your business / client:

For the salesperson

Step 1: data means certainty

Familiarise yourself with key facts about the product or service you are selling. This logical information will provide you with certainty.

Step 2: marketing rapport words

What key red and green words were used in the front-end marketing or by you, the first time you spoke to your prospect? What sparked the prospect's interest in the first place?

Step 3: control your thoughts – hindering or helpful

Replace any hindering thoughts with helpful ones.

Step 4: have a desired outcome

Write down your outcome, what you want, what the next logical step is, and only ask questions directly linked to your outcome. This saves massive amounts of time, and sets your intention.

Step 5: certainty checklist

Go through your certainty checklist questions.

If I were to ring myself, what would I need to hear from me to get to the next logical step?

- What is your OWAC question?
- What tonality will you use?
- What state?
- What objections will you meet?
- What responses will you need?

For the call

Step 6: the first four seconds

You have just four seconds, so make sure your tonality is great and your attitude is right. Write down what you need to do to make that great first impression. Start with the prospect's name – your first name – and business.

Step 7: OWAC Golden Question

Your OWAC question must be linked to your outcome: your real reason for the call, even if it's obvious, and must start with, 'Firstly, thank you for…'

Step 8: power of the pause

Ask a question then STFU. You must stop speaking after a Golden Question.

Step 9: close and stalls

Use the 3As to overcome the first Bank of Bullshit stalls. Make sure you have options to offer.

Step 10: stall or close

Use the 3As for the second time. FOAD is the worst that can happen with this second Bank of Bullshit stalls.

Use the Bullseye Flip Back technique after two stalls, and connect with the positive word used before the stalls to 360 back to the close.

Step 11: money exchange and Sixteen-Digit Close

Prepare your close to get commitment. Remember your language technique: 4Cs (Crisp, Clear, Concise, Certain).

Step 12: thank you and referral

Don't mess about at this point. Thank them, then ask for the referral.

Conclusion

Interestingly, it is helpful to know that even when you and your team have followed my prospecting cycle from start to finish (caterpillar to beautiful butterfly, and Serve, Sell, Close – the Serve Circle) using powerful qualification strategies all along the way and moved the prospect from cold to red hot, even then humans will lie to you, make excuses and buy themselves time. This is the way it works, and you must be prepared for it.

When your prospect has shown an interest in your products or services, and you understand your prospect by knowing:

1. The biggest challenge they have linked to your products or services

2. What they need to solve the challenge

3. That both parties know, like and trust each other

4. There is a strong urgent need to move towards the next logical step and solve the problem or accelerate results

And you have provided your prospect with all the logical information, and you have discussed:

- The possible obstacles

- The possible implications

- The possible risks

- The possible problems

- The prospect's expectations

- Purchasing cultures

- The decision-making process

- Who else is involved in the decision-making process

- That you are talking to the final decision-maker

- That your prospect is emotionally attached to your product or service solving problems and getting even better results (other than just financial wherever possible)

And once a prospect has connected logic and emotion by answering powerful questions linked to your outcome of solving the pain or problems that you created your business to solve in the first place: you know that they know that you know that they know, just go for it – all that is left is to *close* the deal by using this powerful, repeatable, transparent, time-saving and honest system that was designed to get the job done purposefully, professionally and with the right level of persistence.

Remember my simple three-step process for all sales conversations.

QUALIFY – Phase 1

Confirm that you have the correct person.

Wait to hear the tone in their voice.

Transition into Phase 2 – The link is: 'First, thank you...' (transition now).

THEM – Phase 2

Brains 2 and 3: questions where required (Serve, Sell, Close – the Serve Circle).

Thank them for the obvious.

State the purpose of the call or conversation.

Ask a Golden Question.

Stop speaking.

Follow the OWAC system.

Transition into Phase 3 – the link is: 'Here's what I suggest happens next...'

US – Phase 3

Closing questions only (Close cycle).

Lock down the logical next step, to move the situation along your pipeline.

By knowing your exact ending point (Point 4: have a desired outcome) you can ensure that whenever the conversation during Phase 2 feels like it's getting off track, you can ask a question that is linked to your outcome to get back on track (the Christmas Tree strategy, using outcome questions).

Incorporate and master this twelve-point system, and watch not only your conversions rocket through the roof, but your team grow in stature, confidence and communication skills.

It is now your job to implement what you have learned.

A warning from feedback from the many salespeople who have attended my two-day training in Birmingham: you are likely to want to slip back into your old default position, which involves bringing 'No' into play a lot.

Practise every day and ensure that this does not happen.

Check me out on YouTube to get constant reminders.

Visit my landing page for more free training on 'Open With A Close'.

Ask to join my free Facebook community: Elite Closing Academy.

Commit your time and energy into thinking at a higher level about your Prospecting Journey and, crucially, your closing process.

Now, it's over to you.

A few simple reminders

Selling does not need to be underhand, funky or different in any way.

Great selling involves asking powerful questions, and sharing logical and practical information that is helpful to both you and your prospect.

Once you have decided that you are a good match, make a written proposal.

After they have received it, stop selling and start closing.

Set your intention at all times, and be totally transparent. No smoke or mirrors. Your prospects will love you for it, because it quite literally is the opposite of the majority of salespeople out there.

Allow your ancient gifts of understanding both verbal and non-verbal communication and awareness to shine through, allowing yourself to be naturally *you*.

Look to serve by asking, serve by sharing information, serve by selling your products and services and, ultimately, serve by closing those that need your products or services to get even better results or solve problems they have.

Lastly, and most importantly, educate yourself and your team. Get great sales training, role play daily, challenge all the hindering thought processes that we have in sales, and remind yourself of the sales process which, when repeated, gets world-class results.

Become An Elite Closer

Visit www.eliteclosingacademy.com for dates of our training, where you'll learn three key things:

1. About our 12-month Elite Closing Academy Programme

2. A deep dive into the Elite Closing Academy Formula (14 trainings)

3. Leave with your bespoke, twelve-point 'Open With A Close' script to close hot, qualified leads every time.

You will learn everything that you or your team needs to be an Elite Closer, armed with the process, skills, methods, repeatable strategies and techniques to close everything that is closable.

For those that master the life-changing training, life is great because the financial rewards for all your service, knowledge and care come your way, leaving you to serve many more people and prospects without having to worry about sales coming in to pay your bills.

These principles, techniques and tactics are laid out and taught during high-quality sales training for you, your employees and business partners.

The Author

Matthew Elwell is an internationally sought-after sales trainer and mentor, who works with businesses to help their sales function become infinitely more effective.

While spending twenty years building a successful family business, Matthew formulated his own technique when it came to getting deals done (that he used to devastating effect). This is what he calls the 'Open With A Close' philosophy that, in the right hands, is guaranteed to close hot qualified leads every time.

After leaving the family business to follow a passion for serving others, he co-founded the Elite Closing Academy. This was formed for one reason: to give business owners the tools required to make more sales, but in a way that is value driven and not the sleazy, pushy approach many salespeople are tarnished with having.

In a very short space of time, Matthew and the Elite Closing Academy have helped hundreds of UK-based businesses and have now been approached (and hired) by companies in the United States to improve their sales. When it comes to selling, and specifically closing deals, Matthew is fast becoming the number one target for business owners and sales team leaders who want instantly better sales results.

The content of this book is just the start of your journey to finding a better, more fulfilling way of making sales.

Find out more at:

⊕ www.eliteclosingacademy.com

 www.linkedin.com/in/matt-elwell-974943118

▶ www.youtube.com/matthewelwell

 www.facebook.com/groups/eliteclosingacademy

Lightning Source UK Ltd.
Milton Keynes UK
UKHW022106290121
377893UK00007B/236

9 781781 334442